IN THE SHADOWS
DARKLY LIT...

[signature]

10/24/2015

RODNEY A. ROBERTSON

Other books by this author:

Dancing in the dark...My journey into the light.
Published 2013
The Words of the Indigo Angel...
Published 2014

Cover Photograph courtesy of Michael Powell

Authors photo courtesy of Sonya L. King

Email: thelatelordbyron@aol.com

ISBN-13: 978-1516890736
ISBN-10: 1516890736

ACKNOWLEDGMENTS

I wish to give my sincerest thank you and gratitude to Susan E. Deierlein. Her wonderful grammar skills and suggested rewrites helped to give life to this book.

A special thank you needs to be given to Sonya L. King for a suggestion that totally changed the heart of this book.

I want to thank my children, Stephanie and Joshua, for being the lights in my life.

I have to thank my mother, Maryann Robertson, who was the one who taught me what true life strength is. She was one of the strongest individuals I have ever known when it comes to handling so many of life's tests.

For my Grandson, Jasper:

May your world be filled with a Long Life, Laughter and Love!

A word from the Author:

I am a skeptic. I always have been. This is rather ironic since I have been in communication with the dead for as long as I can remember. It's not that I doubt the existence of the spirit world, but that I doubt much of the mythology behind it. In more than thirty years of choosing to walk a paranormal path I have rarely come across trapped spirits, demons or faeries, for that matter.

In my time, I have been inundated with photographs of Orbs that are nothing more that specks of dust, eye lashes or dried skin to the extent that I refuse to even consider photos of orbs as evidence. I have been sent pictures of shadows, animals, faces, reflections and such that are nothing more than matrixed images that the mind sees as whatever the person believes is in the photo. This is not to say that these things do not exist in this universe.

They exist; Ghosts, faeries, demons and things which we cannot explain are on this planet. They exist alongside us in day and night. The spirits of those who have passed tend to "visit" us after they have gone thru through transition from this plane of existence to the next. If we are lucky we can see them thru through photography, shadows or personal experience. We can hear them on occasion and even feel them; or more exactly, they feel us.

In some cases, we feel a spirit's energy in a repetitious cycle or pattern that has imprinted in a room, house or such. The spirit is no longer there but the pattern of its life may still exist in an endless Mobius loop. We feel the energy that is not allowed to vanish in some places because the location becomes a part of urban mythology and people bring their expectations of visiting a haunted site with them. It simply creates an energy which is almost a mental matrixing. Somewhat like mass hallucination; people flock to a site hoping for an encounter and allow a simple noise to become that thing that goes bump in the night.

My goal has always been to seek out what is real in this field of parapsychology. I feel it is extremely important that we maintain a level of skepticism and high standards when processing possible evidence of paranormal activity. I have actually met many competent people in this field. These are the folks who rarely use orbs or such as proof...or, at least know the difference between an orb and a speck of dust.

As you read what is to come I want you to understand that I don't expect anyone who has not experienced these things to believe them. I am a greater skeptic than most of you reading this, but I also know that there are way too many things in this universe that we cannot explain or ignore.

I believe in God. I am a follower of Jesus, Buddha and other spiritual teachers. I believe that we must accept that for all good there is equal bad and that it is a true cosmic balance in which we constantly must make decisions to best follow our own path.

In the end, readers, you will decide to what level you choose to believe these events. In many cases names, locations and such have been fictionalized to protect the privacy of those involved.

PROLOGUE:

Beginnings...

The warm summer rain surrounded us with a heavy mist as we stood in the alley like statues along some forgotten path. They stood there, pale and gray in the shadows darkly lit, drawn to my light. I stood there all alone in a crowd of long dead spirits. The weather didn't bother them and they gave no real regard to the fact that I was soaking wet. What did they care? They couldn't feel it. Death rids you of many common worries. They had become passengers on the ride that was my life and all they were worried about was the final destination. Each spirit was waiting anxiously for their stop; their point of no return. That is, after all, why they had gathered around me.

It felt as though I had been doing this all my life; and perhaps, I have. I really can't remember a time that they did not come to me from their various places in the dark. All through my life I have had exchanges with the spirits and even have guides that are as much a part of me as my

12

own soul. Yeshua was my Birth angel that brought me to earth, and then came Azrael who is one of Deaths emissaries and Pariah the shadow man who is destined to obseve all that is and will be in a person's life; good and evil. There are those I have gathered as a soul family and that I have gathered to help them along their way.

Over the years, I have come to find that I am not alone in gathering souls for both guidance and very often to deliver them to their beyond. They seek out residue energy of near death and/or death moment events. To the roaming spirits on the other side we are something akin to lighthouse beacons shining brightly across the dark empty waters between our world and theirs. The white light energy attracts each and every walking soul; regardless of their temperament.

I tried to fight this aspect of my gift only to find I simply enhanced it and attracted more souls. I have probably done this all my life and have vague recollections of playing with young spirits when I was a child; as though I was babysitting them until it was time to go. As I grew I began to let social knowledge create walls and block them as best I could. I learned early that some things will not be denied.

The rain kept falling as we waited for the Deliverers; the angels that would come to them to guide them beyond the veil. The alley behind the Oriental Theater in Chicago's Theater District across from the Goodman Theater was the perfect spot for us to wait. It had been a site of a great conflagration causing hundreds of deaths; mostly children and their mothers. It was forever marked as a vortex by the depth of the tragic fire. It was a place I could identify with because, like me, it bore spiritual scars.

As the rain came down harder; I stood there slowly fading into the memories of my past...

*****

My first true meeting with Death was when I died in the womb. It was her job to see me through that near premature death while I went through a level of genetic augmentation that I knew was Heaven sent. Because I had much to learn I would not be allowed to remember this event until many years later.

The warm loving comfort of the womb and the safety of being embraced while in the fetal position are beyond compare. It is the only time in my life I recall feeling total unconditional love. The positive energy that flowed into the womb from my mother and the rhythm of her loving heart beat brought nirvana to my soul. I was at peace.

The shock of the white light and the feel of being torn from my fetal body were not even close to the realization that I was standing in some netherworld in my true form of that of a very old soul. My soul self was essentially who

14

I am, always was and who I always will be. I was out of sync at first but as the cloudy mist of this realm parted I began to gain my senses.

"I am Azrael. I am a minion of death. I am a Deliverer. I have brought you here to help you begin your journey. This will be your most difficult lifetime." I turned to see a beautiful woman standing behind. Her reddish brunette hair flowed and floated about as she spoke. "You have a lot of control over this lifetime but you will also have to suffer many lessons, many broken hearts and many disappointments. You will only be gone for a moment in the womb and your mother will know and be alarmed. The quicker we do this the sooner you will return."

"I am confused. I have never had to do this before upon returning to life." This was a new experience to me and I didn't really know what to say or do. "I don't want to hurt my mother so do what needs to be done. She is a good woman and filled with such love. I am ready."

"You have to allow me to empty your memory of all but the things you will need in this lifetime. The memories and thoughts of the past will come forward when you need them. As your life progresses all thoughts I give to you will be brought forward. Never forget that all you receive you receive from the Holiest of Holy. The Universal Is." As she said that she began to cover me in many layers of light, healing colors and thoughts.

I don't remember how much time passed but it felt as though I had been there an eternity. Azrael, an angel of death, had a beauty to her as she went about preparing me for this life ahead. I felt old memories dying and being relegated to some small part of my mind as new thoughts began to fill in the spaces they had left vacant. In those moments I knew the secrets to the universe and in even less time they were buried in my subconscious to await their own birth in the life ahead.

"That is all I can do for now. We will meet again in the future. For now, you have to return and calm your mother. She will tell you about this someday." Azrael seemed tired and sad that I was leaving.

"Are you okay?" I felt some tie to her that seemed to dispell the fear I should have had; this was, after all, death.

"I am fine. You will find that this work can be exhausting on many levels. You will learn to deal with it. Now, you have to be on your way. Your mother and your future are waiting." Having said that she smiled a sweet motherly smile and I felt myself slipping away.

I returned to the womb and immediately felt worry and fear from my mother. I softly shifted my position and gave her a slight kick to let her know all was well. In a few moments the womb refilled with that warmth and love she would always have within her.

*****

My first "friend" was named Yeshua but he had me call him Joshua. He had brought my spirit to earth to live within my mother's womb and be born into this time. We grew up together and I remember games of hide and seek with the occasional race through the house or adventures in camping in the hidden room at the back of my closet.

He was the champion of hide and seeks until I reached the age of five. It was then that he managed to teach me to trust my instincts over what my eyes or ears guided me to. Bit by bit, I began to find him quicker and easier until we finally stopped playing all together.

When I reached the age of five, Yeshua began to introduce me to other "friends" in the neighborhood. I was never alone and we had many adventures around the neighborhood from exploring the woods to playing in the alleys. My new friends all seemed to have some special ability that I would eventually learn to use or at the very least mimic. It never occurred to me at that time that these friends would eventually go away once I had mastered their secrets. The fact is it never even entered my mind that these friends were in reality "Ghosts". It wasn't until I was about six years old that I learned they were not "normal" people.

During a routine game of tag I was hot on the heels of Yeshua when he made a daring move and ran through the wall. I assumed that since I could do everything he did I would go through the wall with ease. He turned sharply into the wall with me following him at full speed. They tell me I hit the wall at a fast run and knocked myself for a loop. My only explanation was that I was following the little boy I was playing with and I thought I could go through the wall as well.

I had to endure a few weeks of being the butt of everyone's jokes until they all realized that I had been serious. I was sent to the doctor to have my head examined and then a psychologist to have my mind examined before I was determined to be sane and "normal." During this time the crowd around me had begun to gather. I awoke one morning around four a.m. to find my bedroom filled with people from all ages and all walks of life; good and evil.

To my knowledge this was the first incidence of my being a gatherer. Over the next few weeks I couldn't sleep and was constantly awakened at four a.m. each morning until I became an insomniac. I couldn't sleep long nor was I ever truly deeply asleep. Yeshua would keep me company during the late nights until one night when I suddenly blanked out. I awoke several hours later well rested and feeling very calm. Yeshua told me I had released the spirits to their guides so they could find their way to their destinations.

From this time on I began to realize I was different from most people. I knew that this was going to happen again and again. I eventually learned to assimilate these events into my "regular" childhood activities. Yeshua tried his best to watch over me and allow me as much of a childhood as possible for someone that had become a gatherer.

*****

I was about 6 years old when I became aware of the things that go bump in the dark. We lived in a multilevel home with just enough rooms for each of us children to share. It was a standard suburban house on a nice lot that was near the school and a few parks. Most of the neighbors were hard working middle class types. It was a typical neighborhood filled with large families who had hidden secrets behind each front door.

I shared a room with my brother who was at best a bully towards me and at worst a cruel tormentor. He made it clear for as long as I could remember that he did not care for me at all. He would constantly hit me or harass me whenever he knew the adults were not near enough to see his misdeeds. He enjoyed every moment of my misery and actually seemed to seek out every chance he could to bully me. He finally had a chance to torture me in the one way he knew would do the most harm.

It happened one autumn when I woke up in the early morning hours and turned on a light to see my way to the bathroom. I was allowed to keep a light on for the most part because I had been having night fears and "seeing" things move about in the dark. My brother would often taunt me by shutting off the light. On this particular night I came back to our room and crawled into bed. My brother took the opportunity to turn the light out on me and leave the room; locking the door behind him.

He taunted me by saying. "Better watch out...the monsters are going to get you!"

I cried out, "Please turn the light on!" My *please* fell upon deaf ears as he walked away down the hallway to the downstairs living room.

I cried as silently as I could and hid under the covers praying the light would come back on. It didn't. Then I noticed the quiet that fell so heavily on the room. I found the courage to peek out from under the covers. Suddenly, I realized that the closet door was open! I always made sure that door was closed before I went to sleep. I hated how it made me feel when the door was opened even a crack. As I sat up intending to run to the door and close it, I was startled by a dark figure at the threshold of the door.

I stopped a moment thinking it was simply shadows or even a coat hanging in the closet.

I called out to the shadows; "Is someone there? Who is it?"

Then, from that darkness, there was a course whispering voice...

"Pariah," it said.

I straightened up and stared into the shadows. Time stood still for a moment until shocking dark eyes glared at me from the doorway. I saw what I came to call the shadow man named Pariah. He came to me as a figure darker than the shadows dressed in a black flowing long coat, black clothes and long white flowing hair. As I put my fear aside to look into his face, I saw a haggardly old man whose cragged albino features cut into my soul by way of his intensely dark black eyes. He was neither evil nor good, but some odd creature more sinner than saint but radiating an energy that seemed to cry out for balance. He was in some odd way true justice.

He stood there like some Fortean Phenomena; an unexplainable enigmatic creature whose only purpose was to bring about and witness the judgment of souls from each side of the veil. I did not realize at that time that I would meet this figure again and again. The long black coat and ebbing white hair became clear as this diminutive albino creature floated slowly out of the closet bringing with it an aura that brought out my fear.

I knew it was not like the others; the angels and spirits I had become aware of around me and those I love. It was neither of Heaven nor Hell; I was both afraid and in awe of this entity. It hovered over me for what seemed like an eternity. And then, I screamed! I told it to go away.

It remained there a moment watching me with its ever darkening eyes in its aged face. I felt its hot breath covering me with the stench of a life too long lived. We stared at each other for what seemed to be forever, and then he simply faded back into the closet. I threw the covers back over my head and curled up in a fetal position until I mercifully fell asleep.

This was my first known contact with anything other than a positive spirit. I have since learned that Pariah was not necessarily his name but his destiny as well. The definition of a pariah is a person who is rejected from society or who is an outcast. In life he had been an outcast and in death he had become outcast among the spirits. I would learn later in life why he was there.

The incident with Pariah was my first known realization that those things we "imagine" in the shadows are real. It was my first true lesson in experiencing what I could sense and in realizing I could actually control what could contact me. I knew then and there that I had to give the entities permission to contact me.

I had the power to embrace their spirit and the power to send them on. I could now sense the newly dead, long dead and those that were here but had never walked the earth. This was also the time for me to accept my guardian angel, Yeshua, who I wrote about previously in my book The Words of the Indigo Angel.

Yeshua was my Life angel. He had brought me to earth to be born, he watched over me when I met Azrael and would stay with me past the time of my death. Later on I would learn that there are spirits of balance and truth that do not fit in man's definition of good and evil.

It has been over 50 years since that encounter with the dark entity and nearly 45 years since my first "walk through" of a house to see what spirits were present. During that time, I encountered many cases that were easily explained by natural or human causes. I have also experienced angels and demons in homes. It is the cases in which I found true activity and events that led me to a final understanding of the albino creature.

CHAPTER ONE:

The Night before Christmas

I was eight years old when we went to my grandparent's house in Arkansas for the holiday. At that time, they lived in an old farmhouse which seemed very dark and scary to a seven year old. It was a white farmhouse with black trim, fairly common to the area and constructed to be filled with many children as was the habit in the old days of large farms. Farmers knew the more children you had the fewer farmhands you had to hire. Grandmother had lost more children than she had given birth to, a fact that filled my grandmother with a somewhat silent grief. My father and my aunt were all that survived. The house was stoic and at times it seemed large and foreboding with too many dark rooms. It had an old musty smell common to farm houses of the time, possibly because this was an era when there were no household cleansers other than bleach, pine oil and whatever the woman of the house felt suited her home. The structure was two stories with a walk-in attic room that gave me chills every time I came near it. This room smelled of forgotten hopes and the mustiness of long lost souls. I had not wanted to go to Arkansas because at that age I feared that Santa would not find where I was and I would not get my gifts. I had been a very good boy that year and was sure that I would reap the rewards of such saintliness. Despite my protest we loaded up the old Chevy station wagon and headed down to Jonesboro, Arkansas.

As the miles began to dwindle away so did the snow. I was horrified at the thought of no snow because it's a known fact Santa needs snow for his sled. This was already a nightmare to my young mind. We pulled up in front of the old dark house in the wee morning hours and were immediately ushered to our rooms to sleep. I was filled with dread as I was directed to the attic room to share with my brothers and sleep on a cot.

As I had said; the room was dark and musty with little light and nearly no air. I could feel something in the room with us but was told to be quiet and go to sleep. I did as any child would do; I covered my head with the blanket and shut my eyes as tight as I could. Despite sensing something standing by me I never moved until the morning and first light. When I heard my mom downstairs I dressed without hesitation and ran to the kitchen.

"You're up bright and early. Did you have the bad dreams again?" Mom always knew.

"It is that room," I said. "It feels yucky. I see "them" all around and I can't sleep."

"Did you remember the song I taught you…The hymn that you learned to sing to protect you?" Mom taught me the song, Onward Christian Soldiers, as a way to shield myself against the dark figures that walked in the shadows of my nights.

"I sang it to myself and put the covers over my head. They left me alone and I fell asleep." I quickly added, "But, it wasn't real sleep. I kept waking up and heard them breathing and walking around the room!"

"They can't hurt you as long as you believe in God." The way mom spoke made me believe it with every fiber of my being, and it comforted me for a while.

The day went by quickly with visits from other relatives, food and children's games. I loved walking outside on the farm even though we were warned to stay by the house. The road in front was what passed as a main highway at the time, and on this holiday eve it seemed as busy as a Chicago street. That was ok by me because I loved to explore the old sheds and the barn. A farm is a wonderful place for a kid to grow up with its many hiding places and adventures. It was dinner time before I knew it.

At dinner there was a lot of discussion over who had died recently, what the county was doing to farmers, and the state of the country. Those things did not affect me as I was more concerned with the chicken dinner, mashed potatoes, biscuits and desserts that filled the dining table.

Mom, Grandmother and Aunt Ella were masters of southern cooking. Southern fried chicken, stuffing, beans, and of course, that delicious German Chocolate Cake that grandmother cooked to perfection drew my attention throughout the meal.

After dinner we all sat around the fireplace and listened to stories of the old days and remembered those no longer living. (I have to say, however, that they were still present with us at that gathering.) It wasn't long before the youngest of us were sent to bed or told we would face the wrath of Santa for not being asleep when he arrived. I stalled for as long as I could, then I turned to my brothers as if to say, "Ok, let's get some sleep." They were not going; since they were older, it was not mandatory for them to go to bed when I did.

Mom walked me up to that attic room and sat for a few minutes singing me to sleep. When it didn't work she smiled and kissed my forehead then tucked me in. I was alone.

The light snapped off with a thunderous click, and I lay there in the dark. The only light present was what managed to seep through the curtains hung loosely on the singular small window at the other side of the room. It simply seemed to illuminate every nook of the room in an almost dark light. I stared into the dark for a moment but then, as usual, my "gift" kicked in, and I watched as the shadows slowly began their dance macabre. They came to life in the shadows darkly lit like some silent family coming together for the night's revelry.

I was alone in this room filled with spirits who had once inhabited the land and the house itself. I was terrified! I tried to scream out but had no voice. Fear had frozen my vocal chords and nearly paralyzed me. I covered my head under the blankets and began to sing that old hymn I had learned. It was my wall against them; my draw bridge that would always keep them from getting too close. On a night I should have fallen to sleep dreaming of Christmas gifts and grand foods; I cried myself to sleep with silent tears and that hymn singing in my head.

It was just after midnight when I woke up to an odd energy standing in the room. I saw what looked like a red coat and jacket and sat up in hopes of getting a good look at Santa.

"Santa!!! Is that you" I cried out with glee.

Suddenly I heard an empty voice in my head say, "Yes, dear boy, there is a Santa...but not here. Not now."

The red façade faded to gray, then black, and I realized I was seeing Pariah; that shadow man from a year earlier, the creature that seemed to lurk on the darkest edge of night time waiting to invade my sleep.

His dark, empty eyes came closer, and then he leaned over me dragging breath that seemed to smell of long dead emotions.

I found my voice and screamed as loud as I could! He smiled as though my scream was a sign he truly existed. As my brothers jumped up and the light came on he faded away leaving me to my parents' and family's insistence that it had all been a dream...a nightmare.

CHAPTER TWO:

Chautauqua Preacher

The next year on a warm spring day my grandmother took me to a Chautauqua Tent Revival. I wasn't sure what the hell a Chautauqua tent was much less a revival meeting. My Irish Grandma Louise was throwing a High Holy Fit when Grandma Pauline came to get us so I figured it couldn't be all bad. I looked to Yeshua to see if he was going but he simply declined and went away to where ever it is he would go to. These days, more often than not, I found myself on my own without his company or guidance.

We drove to a small grove of trees in a beautiful park just outside of town. The tent was set up further along inside the park. As we neared it, I remarked that it was the same sized tent we had seen at the Barnum Bailey circus. Grandma was not amused.

As we headed toward the tent, we walked almost en masse with a group of people who had arrived by bus. They were devoted followers of the main speaker and never missed her sermons. All the way in I listened to their exhortation of hellfire and brimstone preaching and justifiable indignation towards the wicked.

We entered the tent after depositing our dollar "donation" with a young girl who smelled of honeysuckle and wore a wonderful light rose colored dress perfect for a warm summer's day. She smiled at me and said, "Well now here's an earth angel if ever I saw one!"

She spoke with an accent I had never heard before, and yet, it seemed as though I had heard it a million lifetimes ago. My grandmother explained to me that it was a Cajun Creole accent and that the girl and her mother were from Louisiana.

We found our seats behind the minister's bus load of the faithful who sounded a bit like of Deadheads for Gospel. We sat on long hard wood benches. I noticed more than a few produced soft pillows from bags and purses to survive the furor yet to come.

After less than ten minutes the entrance to the tent was closed and a light began to shine on the makeshift stage holding up a grand podium. A rather striking woman walked onto the stage as though to introduce the speaker. For some reason it did not surprise me when this almost perfectly sculpted woman began to deliver a sermon that stays with me until this day.

She spoke softly at first in lilted tones that reminded me of a soft whisper in the wind. Her smile and warm eyes seemed to hypnotize me. She talked of the future and how there would be a day when speaking the word of God in a tent would no longer be allowed or may well be made extinct by wealthy churches and government bureaucracy. She lamented that too often if a lay preacher or independent minister did not have a building to call a church then they would not be given the respect they deserved. She promised to continue her way of preaching until her last breath. And then...The Heavens greeted us with her words and rained fire.

My emotions ran from fulfilled and powerful to small and scared. I heard promises of salvation and the threat of damnation. She looked at each and every soul there and made sure that each was tended to. She reached out not to convert but to heal. She cried when she talked to the woman whose husband had died in a car accident leaving her and her small child poor. She smiled with pride and hope when she was reminded of her great efforts by one of the Tent Bus Groupies. She walked amongst those seeking some sign of hope and healing and saw to it that each received a blessing. Then she stopped in front of me.

She looked at my Grandma and said, "Is this the one? Is he your grandson? Is he the one that sees angels?" My grandma stood proud and defiant and acknowledged me. I sat there bewildered and humbled that this great woman carrying the visage of an angel herself knew of me. I was the boy that saw spirits.

She pulled me onto the stage and instructed me to sit in a chair on stage. I was almost nine years old and really scared. I did as I was told. She walked about choosing people and they stepped up to the stage. Then without as much as a by your leave she began to glow this marvelous color, some gold and some silver...some blue and some red...some black and some white.

She looked at the souls before her and began to heal them. Ear issues...healed. Eye issues... healed. Health issues too numerous to mention...healed. I sat and watched as each soul shivered and fainted and danced with new found freedom and faith. Then she ended the sermon with a simple request..."Be at peace."

As the crowds began to disperse she invited my Grandma and me to join her back stage. I was in a spiritual daze. This woman was some grand Saint come to earth to save us all. How wrong Grandma Louise had been. This woman was Heaven sent.

I sat there as she talked to my grandma and told her of a few different people who might help me with my gift. She turned to the young girl we met at the entrance, "This is my daughter Adrienne Dimanche. Adrienne this young man is Rodney Robertson. "We shook hands but there was a sense that we both wanted to hug each other. "Adrienne, get this young man some lemonade and cookies."

"Yes, mother." I noticed as Adrienne moved, she was filled with beautiful glowing energy. In that moment, I felt as though we had met a thousand times before in a thousand lifetimes.

"Rodney, your life is going to be very different from most folks." Her deep southern accent seemed to flow gently across the room. "You really are special and need to be patient. You have a lot of life ahead of you."

Adrienne returned with my refreshments. "Here you go."

"Thank you." I suddenly got shy. For a moment Adrienne and I shared a glance.

"It was nice to meet you." Adrienne seemed to know something I did not. "See you later." The minister smiled at her as she left the tent.

"Just remember that as long as you keep your Faith you will do the right thing. There will be times when you are confused and question all of it. Good. It will keep you honest." With that she smiled and walked us to the tent entrance.

"Have faith in yourself and your gift. Never settle for a simple explanation or someone other person's opinion of your life."

After a few more minutes we left the evangelist standing at the entrance to her sanctum...all aglow.

Suddenly, I knew I had to say something to her and ran back to her. I said simply, "It won't hurt."

" I know." She hugged me, and as I walked away she said, "No matter what, remember that in our darkest moments we get the greatest gifts!"

I have remembered that all my life; and in times when my soul was ready to empty itself of all caring, it saved me. Grandma and I drove back in silence that day. I was sitting there wondering why she had brought me to the tent when she was so against what I did. Perhaps she knew at that point I had no control over my abilities or maybe I was allowed to see a part of her I would never get to see again. Either way, this grandma never again acknowledged my gift and often decried it as black magic. And yet, she had introduced me to my first Light worker.

I realized then that I wasn't alone or odd. And years later I realized that Grandma Pauline had been given the same gift as me and perhaps felt I should have the chance to use it. Why she was afraid to use her own gifts I will never understand.

The minister came back to the area several more times over the next few years, and I always seemed to find a way to catch the train or bus to see her. Adrienne wasn't with her.

Adrienne had gone to stay with her grandmother somewhere in the south. The minister's name was Reverend Alice Sunday. She died of lung cancer at the age of 40, four years after I met her. I learned that I was not alone, and I was not the devil and that someday I would be carrying on a great tradition. It would take me a few years more to actually believe it though.

CHAPTER THREE:

The boy in the woods

That very next summer we went camping at the Lake in the Pines campground located near Ladysmith, Wisconsin. Dad had purchased an old army barracks style tent for us to sleep in. Then he built a big wooden storage trailer reminiscent of a wagon train's grub wagon on top of what had been a flatbed hauling trailer. He managed to fit just about everything inside of it, hitched it up, and pulled it behind our old Chevy Station Wagon.

The campground was a family favorite we went to at least twice a year. This was back in the day when the sites were more private and surrounded by trees. It was perfect for our large family, including various relatives that came along on our trips.

We would usually leave for camp as soon as dad got home from work and rested up. For the most part we would stop only for dinner. The ride wasn't usually too bad once we got under way. Everyone settled in talking or reading to while away the time. Our first stop was a diner in Pittsville, Wisconsin. It was a quaint place that boasted "home cooked" meals and a welcoming atmosphere. On each table sat a miniature juke box and the typical table accessories common to diners of the day.

I looked forward to our visits here because it was the only place I had ever known that sold Pizza Burgers! I was addicted to them. They always seemed to be that one thing that made the start of vacation official. We enjoyed this diner not only because of the familiar pizza burgers, but also because getting there meant we were halfway to the campground.

We generally arrived at Lake in the Pines early in the morning and quietly set up our tent. While the men were busy doing this, Mom and the girls would start breakfast and get the area set for our stay. Food cooked on a campfire is always delicious but when you add Mom's wonderful talent for cooking it became a feast. The smell of bacon, sausage, eggs, biscuits and gravy filled the air along with that wonderful smell of a campfire.

Once we were all set up and had eaten it was time to go down to the lake for some fishing and, eventually, a swim at the beach. As we walked towards the water we were met by the park ranger who chatted with my dad for a moment. While they were talking I noticed a boy about my age standing at the edge of the woods. He was wearing a bathing suit and dripping wet which was odd since it was an unseasonably cool morning. He waved at me and then walked back into the woods.

We each found our spot along the shore and cast our lines out. Mom had made a special point of having me sit near her and it seemed that if I began to wander even a bit she would tell me to stay close. I finally gave in and took a seat just down from her within eye sight. Once I got comfortable I realized I had company. The boy from the edge of the woods was sitting nearby.

He looked at me at first and smiled. "Hello. I'm Danny."

"Hi! I'm Rod." I was overjoyed to have someone my own age there to talk to. "Wish I could go swimming. It's going to be a hot day, but we have to fish first."

"It's cold. My mommy tried to warm me up with a blanket but it didn't work. I think she cried." Danny seemed to be looking out in the distance across the water at an old cabin on the other side of the lake. "That's my house. Mom and dad don't live there anymore."

"Do you live with your grandparents?" I think I already suspected the answer that was coming.

"No. They died a long time ago. I am by myself." Danny glanced away towards his cabin again but in a somewhat somber way.

"Are you dead?" I lacked the finesse of an adult and as such spoke honestly with him.

"I think so. I have been here for a year and no one talks to me. My grandpa visits me and tries to get me to go home with him, but I have to wait for my mommy. She told me not to go away." I think he really wanted to go with his grandpa but didn't want to make his mother cry again. I understood how he felt.

"Do you want to help him?" I was startled at first but quickly realized that Yeshua was with us.

"Yes. Can we? He seems so lonely." As I spoke I saw a somewhat familiar woman standing by Danny. "Is that his mom? Is she here for him?"

"No, that is not his mother. He belongs to her now. He will be okay. Things will happen today, and he will be free to go with his grandpa." Yeshua always came to me in the way I could best understand, and in this case he was like a grandpa.

I looked at Danny and told him it was okay. "You're going to be fine now. You get to go home with your grandpa."

"Thank you! I'm not cold anymore." He suddenly sat up and smiled. "Mommy is home; I can see her from here."

I looked across the lake and saw there was a group standing by the water as though in prayer.

"Goodbye, Rod. Thank you!" With that, Danny walked into the woods with the woman until he joined up with an older man who I realized immediately was his grandfather.

I looked at Yeshua and asked what was going on across the lake.

"They found Danny's body a year ago after he had drowned and today is the memorial for him. His mother has come to terms with her loss. They are releasing his ashes into the lake because he loved it here so much. The cabin belonged to his grandfather and they will live there together."

"How did I help him?" I was clueless.

"He knew you could see him and he needed to be grounded to this spot so she could reach him. Until you came along he couldn't stand still for long. You talked to him. It gave him time to center his spirit and focus on where he needed to go. You gave him the energy he needed. That's part of your gift."

I gave Yeshua a hug and then ran over to where my mom was sitting. I gave her a big hug and told her I loved her! She gave me a bigger hug and said she loved me too! I stayed close to mom all day. We found out later that the park had closed the beach for the day out of respect for Danny's family.

CHAPTER FOUR:

Campfire Stories

It is a time honored tradition to tell ghost stories around a campfire; my family was no different. My mom had grown up in a small town in Alabama named Athens. She was part of a large family that traveled around the country planting and picking harvest for large farms. Mom told us two stories from one of the places they lived that stay with me to this day.

Mom grabbed a cup of coffee and her cigarettes as she got comfortable in her lawn chair sitting just close enough to the campfire to take the chill off the night air. She talked a bit about how they had been living in an old house at the base of a hill near a river and close to the school. They lived a modest life and often made do with what the world made available to them.

"We were not rich by any means but Daddy made sure we had food to eat and dressed nicely. We lived in nice houses and worked hard in the fields. We would attend school as much as possible and Momma raised us well." Mom stopped a moment to sip coffee and take a puff or two of her cigarette.

"When we were younger my sister Cassie who was the twin of my sister Catherine got sick. She was so sick that they put her in the room with Momma and daddy. Each day her condition worsened and everyone was afraid she would not make it." Mom seemed to stare off into the past for a moment.

"One night, when Cassie was the worst she had been, Daddy told Momma to go sit for a bit and rest. Momma went out to the kitchen to get some coffee and pie before she would rest for a few hours. As she stood at the sink filling the coffee pot from the pump she saw a man standing at the top of the hill by an old oak tree.

"Suddenly, out of nowhere lightening hit the tree and it burst into flames. A huge ball of flames began to roll down the hill towards the house. Momma was startled as the ball of fire slammed into the front door with a loud crash. She yelled for Daddy to come in, and as he rushed in she ran to him yelling that the door was on fire. He stopped a moment, saw that the door was fine, and told her she had been exhausted and dreamed the whole thing. Your grandma finally calmed down and went to bed.

"The next morning, Grandma awoke to find that Cassie had come out of her sickness. It was like some miracle. She rushed about the house letting everyone know the good news. Everyone began to emerge from their rooms as Mama reached the last room where Catherine was asleep. She opened her door and called to her about her twin sister. She didn't answer. Mamma walked over to the old feather bed to shake her awake only to find that she had died in the middle of the night."

Mom stopped a moment as we all gasped at that revelation.

"Later when they tore apart that feather bed they found something strange. It was what looked to be a crown of feathers as though a sign from God that this was meant to be. Momma still has that crown to this day."

We all sat a moment to think about Mom's story and to give her time to get another cup of coffee and a cigarette.

"We had a lot of odd things happen in that old house. A few years later, we had a chance to go down to the playground by the local school. The quickest way to get there was along the river, and Momma made it clear we had to be home before dark.

"We all headed to the playground hand-in-hand anxious to have some fun. We ran into other kids from the area and soon went about doing things with our friends from school. We had so much fun that we forgot the time and before we knew it the sun was setting.

"Your Aunt gathered us all together and made sure we held each other's hands. She also gave us a stern warning to not look back behind us or at the river. We marched quickly along the river as night time fell giving way to all of the noises of the night. Your aunt made sure each of us went towards the house in front of her, and when we arrived at the door she made sure we were all inside first.

"My daddy noticed something was wrong and stepped outside with your aunt. He asked her what was wrong. She told him that when we left the playground she noticed a woman in black following us. When she got to the river she seemed to float on it and follow us all the way home. Daddy walked down to the river to see if he could see this woman but had no luck. He couldn't explain it, and to this day it is a mystery."

With that my mom sent us all to our sleeping bags for a good night sleep. The one thing about her story that has stuck out for me has always been the description of the floating lady. It was identical to the woman I had seen taking Danny to his Grandpa!

CHAPTER FIVE:

Angels, Death and the Shadow Man

When I was just a little over nine years old I had my very first brush with puppy love. Her name was Cheryl, and she was my first kiss. She reminded me of Adrienne in ways and I was drawn to her beautiful energy. In a moment of youthful curiosity we snuck away to a bathroom while at her house and kissed each other right smack on the lips!

"Let's kiss!" Cheryl said. We had grown up together and I would do anything for her.

I puckered up, and for a quick moment our lips touched. We tried it again. I don't know what we thought was going to happen, but all I remember after that kiss was getting caught and yelled at. If it had not been for her younger siblings we would have gotten away with our innocent little tryst.

Needless to say we were severely chastised for our stolen moment; our sweet, warm and wonderful kiss that to this day still lies softly on my lips. It was my first non-maternal love.

The spring was a warm one and Cheryl and I had become an item. No more kissing though, because, we were not ready to raise that family our parents had warned us of. We played each day and usually had lunch together. The perfect couple; we were too busy for others. Even Yeshua, my angelic guide and companion, understood our love as he chose to stay away and only come out to play when I was on my own.

One rather perfect spring day, my friend Tiger came by to play and immediately fell head over heels for Cheryl. I was devastated! He began to display his expertise with the various tricks one could execute on a banana bike. I was crushed.

He came on strong by riding his bike with no hands on the handle bars! I could barely ride the darn thing. I had never done much more than master the fine art of actually staying on the bike. Tiger was a pint sized Evil Knievel. She was smitten!

"Isn't Tiger cool? I love his bike. Did you see him pop that wheelie?" Cheryl had become a one girl cheerleading squad for my old friend and new nemesis.

"Big deal; anyone can do that!" These were brave words from someone who had never quite mastered the fine art of the wheelie.

"I bet he can do anything!" Cheryl had finally pushed my buttons. It was time to bring out my A Game.

I knew I had to do something big. I had to perform one of my greatest feats ever! This was no time for cheap gimmicks and fancy showmanship. I had to bring out my inner daredevil. I had to shine brighter than I had ever shined before. I was ready. I had formulated the perfect stunt that even the insurgent Tiger would not attempt.

I would stand up and ride my bike!

I would get a running start and ride triumphantly out of my garage with arms rose reaching to the sky! I would sweep her off her feet like Roy Rogers at a rodeo!

I shook off my fear. I took several deep breaths. I was ready to go.

And then, I looked over and Yeshua was there looking at me...shaking his head. Then... he disappeared.

Despite Yeshua's obvious disapproval of such a fool's maneuver, I had a woman to win and so...

Ready! Set! Go!

I got a great start! My bike was true to my aim. I waited a moment, and at the right time I stood tall and proud upon my bike. As I neared the open garage door, I raised my hands in the truest showman form! I was in all of my glory.

It was then that I saw the dark creature in black standing in the shade under the old willow tree at the end of the driveway. His dark empty eyes burned into my soul and all my fears seem to well up inside me. I hardly noticed my thumb being sliced by the rusty and dirty garage door frame. The dark man faded away.

Cheryl ran to me as I came crashing to the ground.

"Oh, my gosh! Are you okay?" She was deeply upset.

"I am fine. I didn't feel a thing!" I was going to be brave no matter how much I wanted to cry.

"You're bleeding!" She screamed as she pointed at the blood running from my hand.

Apparently my flawless ride was in truth an accident waiting to happen. I hit the garage floor fast and hard; my hand bleeding profusely. I had in a much unplanned way won her heart again. What woman can resist a wounded warrior? She tended to my wound and nursed me all the way until she had to go home for dinner.

I remained on my field of honor for a few minutes more. I was afraid I would get in trouble for this unnecessary injury! I was sure that I had finally committed my last infraction. The mind of a nine year old is sometimes a scary thing; especially to the nine year old.

And then, for the first time, I was mad at Yeshua. He knew these things would happen and always warned me. It's why I lived such a charmed life. He always was there to protect me. How could he let me get hurt like that? He didn't even have the decency to show himself!

I was certain the Shadow man had caused this. He had been watching from the shade and made sure I would fail. Why hadn't Yeshua protected me from him?

It wasn't until a few days later that I had my answers. I also died...again.

A nine year old boy can be pretty clever when he needs to be. I found a variety of ways to hide the wound to my thumb. In fact, had it not been for the blood infection that had set in I would have gotten away with my fear based deception. Yeshua had not shown up at all, and I must admit to being somewhat lost.

It took about three or four days before the fever started. Mom thought at first that it was a summer cold and treated it accordingly. A few days passed before the dizziness set in. The fever wouldn't go away, and I was growing weaker. My feverish mind seemed intent on allowing the dark creature to "live" in my head. It got so bad that Mom decided to keep me home from school one more day.

Mom asked a neighbor to check on me during the day as she had to go to work. I was alone for most of the day. It was at this time that I saw the dark creature across the room and first noticed the woman dressed in black standing next to him. It was the woman in the woods!

She was a young woman, not quite 40, with reddish brunette hair and glistening milky white skin. Her eyes were filled with a somewhat sad and forlorn wisdom. It was as though she was waiting for me to come to her. Behind her stood the shadow man with his glowing dark black eyes watching it all as though waiting for some great cosmic shift.

That afternoon, mom came home early. She took my temperature and began to search my arms for red streaks...she found them. I could barely stand as she dressed me and whisked me to the doctor's office. I remember her comforting hand sweeping gently across my forehead as we sat waiting for me to be seen. I was taken in rather quickly and the doctor was expedient in his diagnosis. In the shadows of the doctor's dimly lit examining room stood a dark figure that vanished as I became aware it was there.

I lay on the examining table as the doctor told my mother I had blood poisoning.

"He is dying and needs immediate treatment around the clock. If we don't start treating him within two hours he may die within the next 72 hours!" The doctor had no time to be delicate or worry about the effect saying this in front of me might have.

"I don't want to die, Mommy!" I started to cry.

"You are NOT going to die!" My mom looked at the doctor and told him he was wrong. She said that he needed to tell the hospital I was on my way!

We left the doctor's office and drove back home so Mom could call my dad and grab some clothes for me. We pulled into the driveway and were met by the neighborhood kids. I told them that the doctor said I was going to die. Everyone began to cry. Cheryl's mother was there. She became the calming voice by telling them I would be ok and they would see me soon.

They all hovered around the car waiting for Mom to return to take me to the hospital. Standing a little behind them was that lady who had visited earlier; offering neither voice nor movement...just watching over me.

The folks at the hospital met us at the emergency entrance and brought me quickly to my room where I was immediately adorned with a variety of medical apparatus, machines and IVs. Nurses were briefed and interns brought in to witness the procedures that I would go through. Shots were given around the clock at fifteen minute intervals. This would continue for days.

It was on the fourth day that I died. I remember all of the doctors and my parents were gathered there talking about what needed to be done next. I was too young to understand the technical jargon and, in truth, wasn't interested. I was dying and I knew it.

There were too many angels roaming about the room; stopping to look at me a moment as though curious as to why I was able to see them. Some would attempt to speak but would be hushed by others. The room had a peculiar glow to it. Suddenly, they all went silent and quickly left the room.

SHE had begun to walk towards my bed and they feared her. That woman who had stood near me a few days earlier had shown up again. She stopped as they cleared the room and glanced only once towards the people holding conference at the foot of my bed. It was then that I realized the shadow man was standing by them...observing.

I was scared. I wanted to cry but couldn't. I didn't want to scare Mom or make her cry anymore. As I was lying there alone in a room full of people, the woman in the shadows moved toward me from where she had been standing so silently. She came to my bed, and it was at that moment I knew she was Death. And then... Death sat upon my bed.

She looked at me as a mother would an injured child. "Do not be afraid. It really doesn't hurt. Soon you will be with people who know you and love you. They will take care of you."

I was sad. I knew my mom, standing a few feet away, would be hurt when I left and that was more than I could bear. I was nine years old and she was my "mommy". She believed in me when no one else did. She lifted me up when I was down and carried me when I couldn't go on. She was my heart and soul.

And then.... I died.

Death was gentle and lifted my soul from my body as softly as a whisper. I looked into her eyes and saw such sadness and loneliness. I looked deeper within her and realized that Death was alone in a way that I understood.

"It's only a moment," she whispered. "I promise you will not be alone."

"Will I stay with you? Will you be my new mommy?" It was an innocent question from one so young.

"No. You have to join your family here." She spoke in a reassuring tone.

"You are all alone. I can stay with you. No one should be alone." I asked, "Do you have children? "

She said, "I have had many children but none were allowed to stay."

I said that made me sad, and I would stay with her if she wanted. She cried.

I looked over to Mom and realized that no one had yet realized I had died. Time was different on this side. The mere tick of the clock had passed for them and yet I had been gone for what felt like an hour.

I looked at the bed. My body lay there still and serene. It was then that I noticed Yeshua and the shadow man standing quietly next to my bed. Yeshua looked at me and smiled that smile he has that tells me things are not what they seem and that it will be alright. He stepped over and began talking to Death. The Dark Creature glanced at me; then he vanished.

Yeshua and Death talked for a few moments; then she came to me.

"It isn't your time, and you have things to do." She told me I had died in the womb and Yeshua had come to earth to breathe life back into me and help me make it through. "Indigo Angels are guides of the higher order, and Yeshua is one on high. He is part of the Universal Is."

We talked for a bit more and she gave me things I would need to know throughout my life. (Many of these things have come to me in their own time). She looked over to Yeshua and smiled and then....my fever broke. She kissed me on the forehead and softly faded away into the dark.

Yeshua stayed with me for the next few days as I began to grow healthier and healthier. In these days, he explained that miracles were not without some level of cost. It was about balance, and I would come to understand this as I grew older. I would come to understand both the depth of darkness and the unending piercing lightness of being. Since this event I have chatted with Death on several occasions. I eventually learned she was called Azrael. No matter why she appeared she always acted like a mother to me, even when she came to take my dearest mother across the veil.

CHAPTER SIX:

The Great Vacation

The summer following my near death experience brought my family to the time when we would take our last family vacation together. My dad had decided on a trip across country and took extra time so we could enjoy the trip more. Traditionally family vacations were camping in Wisconsin or along various rivers in Illinois with all of us in an old military mess tent that was big enough to fit the whole family.

On this trip we brought along a pop-up camper filled with everything we would need for a three week adventure across the country. This was a great trip for me as, for the most part, I was surrounded by family and would have things to do... just in case Yeshua came along for the ride. As it turned out, I am glad he did.

For my family this was the trip to end all trips. My oldest brother was due to go to Vietnam and my other brother would follow. A cross country trip was a great adventure for a nine year old, and I couldn't wait to depart.

I remember being woke up early in the morning before the crack of dawn. Dad liked to leave before the traffic got heavy. He liked to leave when we were all sleepy because then we were quiet. Either way, it was always neat to wake up so early on a summer day and head out to parts unknown. The morning was brisk for a summer day and there was the hint of dew on the ground; it was exhilarating and refreshing. I marveled at the morning stars shining above that created a magical moment in my memory.

On this trip we spent a lot of time traveling through some pretty spiritual and holy Native American grounds. Long before I had learned that I was seeing spirits and had a sense of wandering souls. This journey had lessons for me and jumpstarted my life long wanderlust. I had learned to trust in Yeshua and allow him to act as my guide and mentor. This trip was the beginning of our spiritual journey.

As we left Hoffman Estates, Illinois to head west I tried my best to stay awake and watch the world go by along the highway. We traveled down Bode Road passing the old abandoned farm house and rounding the curve that marked the path down to Bode Lake. It wasn't long before we reached the old manor house that always reminded me of Tara from *Gone with the Wind*. It was at this point that I usually fell blissfully asleep.

I awoke somewhere in Iowa as we stopped at a restaurant for breakfast, gas and the necessary potty breaks. It was a typical truck stop diner along the highway with its colorful trucks and even more colorful, truckers. I think Dad may have wished he was a trucker because he always seemed to be looking down the road. Wanderlust is genetic in my family, I believe.

We boarded the old Chevy wagon and assumed our spots for the next phase of our journey. Dad had destinations in mind and would not stop for anything in between. He had a schedule to keep. He found out, however, that it's true what they say about the "best laid plans of mice and men." Too many people in such a confined space made stops necessary whether he liked it or not.

We pulled over into an extremely old rest stop with a small store at the edge. We all took care of our bathroom needs and wandered over to the store. We each got twenty-five cents to spend and could keep what was left over. I did not like this shop. It smelled of decay and old dreams never realized. The old man inside the store seemed to not want children there and made it quite clear that we needed to buy things and stand outside. This place reminded me of every horror movie I had ever seen with the creepy old store. We didn't stay long. I didn't like the spirits that seemed to hang ominously in that store. They seemed trapped one moment then deviously happy to be there. As we drove away I saw the shadow man standing in an upper room looking out the window.

When we arrived at the rest stop just near the foot of Devils Tower we found out that the campground we were headed to was full up. Being a resourceful type, my father found a way for us to stay at the rest stop for the night. He backed the camper into a parking spot and we set up camp for the evening.

Somehow we captured a fire ring and the entire family sat around the fire singing and talking about life. We were not alone.

As we relaxed by the fire roasting marshmallows for s'mores, I became aware that the spirits of many who had passed away had noticed the fire and came to see what was happening. My spirit guide, Yeshua, had shown himself to me. I knew that he would protect me from anything bad. When the spirits began to appear Yeshua welcomed them and explained what was going on.

He took a moment and pointed me out to several of these earthbound angels.

I finally asked," Why are you doing such a thing? Why are they here?"

He explained, "They were drawn more to you than the fire. Having died and come back you are now a sort of beacon to the spirits on the other side. They will always seek you out."

"What about the shadow man? Why is he always showing up?" I figured this was as good a time as any to ask.

"You will understand it all when the time is right." He smiled softly and vanished.

I sat there watching this incredible parade of souls until I was approached by two young spirits; a Native American brother and sister near my age that had died in a massacre and were curious as to this creature that glowed to them and wore such odd clothing. This was an event that I refer to as my first true conversation with the spirits.

His name was Setangya, and his sister was called Memdi. They told me their names and we spoke as children might...despite the fact that they spoke in one of the dead Lakota languages. (Yeshua had already explained to me that when there is a connection it creates a zone in which everything is equal. All languages are one just as all energy is balanced. I would understand this better in the future.)

"We died many years ago. The Comanche raided our village to get horses. When they arrived the elders were hunting in the mountains." Setangya spoke as though he was weary of memories he had carried for decades.

"When they found no horses there and knew the warriors had all gone on the hunt they slaughtered those of us remaining in camp." Memdi spoke as though she was much older than her years.

"When the warriors returned they thought the long knives had attacked the village and sought revenge. They were among the numbers at the Little Big Horn," Setangya spoke.

We talked for a while but soon it was time to go to sleep, so I bid the spirits farewell and went off to lie down. To be honest, I didn't sleep a wink. I had just spoken to "ghosts!" As I tried to drift off to sleep I kept zoning and meeting other spirits... pioneers, soldiers, Indians and more. Suddenly, I realized they were sharing their stories in broken words and sentences... an event that my young mind was not fully able to comprehend. The dreams ended abruptly when the shadow man appeared and they all left. My mind shifted to dream mode and he was pushed away.

Morning came quickly with the sound of my father waking everyone up as quietly as possible. There was some quiet urgency to having us get up and break camp. We rushed about and quickly had everything in place so my father could reconnect the camper to the station wagon. He pulled out of the spot, and as we climbed into the car I noticed we had blocked a sign that read "No overnight parking or camping."

My father had purposely blocked the sign and was now sneaking out before sunrise to avoid possible fines. As we pulled away the owner of the camper next to us stepped out of his camper and saw the sign. What panic ensued we will never know!

We spent a great deal of time in Yellowstone and the Black Hills Area. I was now able to create the zone and speak with spirits on a more regular basis if I chose. When Yeshua was in the mood I would see entire scenarios involving cowboys and Indians. Events played out as my family took tours around the area. The feelings and emotions of such places as Custer's Last Stand at the Little Big horn stay with me to this day. The small towns we would stop in for lunch or a pop or to see some tourist attraction all had history and long dead spirits waiting to share their stories.

It was on this trip that I began learning to overcome my religious and social conditioning in order to focus on this amazing gift I had been given. I was learning to break away from the person society thought I should be to create the person I would become. This did come at a cost as Yeshua had warned…including the fact that while he would always be with me in spirit and guidance; he would not be physically around as much.

CHAPTER SEVEN:

Losing my Spiritual Virginity

I was fourteen when I took my first official walk-through in that abandoned farm on Bode Road in Hoffman Estates Illinois. I had ridden my bicycle past this old home countless times on my way to Bode Lake to fish.

The house had once been a sturdy mail order home. It had been purchased straight out of the Sears Roebuck Catalogue and shipped there by rail and trucks. These homes were fairly common as they were inexpensive and came in many varieties. It was a standard three bedroom home with a large country kitchen in the back. In the front of the house there was a staircase near the front door and a nice fireplace in the living room.

This particular home had belonged to a young couple that had purchased some farm land with the intention of raising a family. WWII came along and dashed those hopes. The husband went to war and never returned. The wife returned to her home town. I could never find out exactly what had happened but the house eventually was abandoned and slowly fell into disrepair.

On one particularly hot summer day as I rode my bike slowly past I heard what sounded like a dog whimpering. I stopped and listened for a few minutes until I was sure that I had indeed heard what sounded like an injured dog. I called out and whistled to see if the poor thing would come to me. Finally, I left my bicycle by the street and slowly made my way along the fence line until I found the gate and walkway towards the house.

There was a soft breeze rustling the tree leaves about in a way that sounded more like waves on the shore than leaves above me. I slowly walked up the stairs to the porch which reminded me of something out of the book *To Kill a Mockingbird*. I half expected Boo Radley to step out of the shadows. I reached the open doorway with its long broken-in door and called out to see if anyone was there who might need help.

"Hello? Is anyone here?" I called out.

In a quick moment everything stopped; the wind died down, the whimpering ceased, and even the birds went quiet.

I could hear my heart beating. My breath seemed labored as the sweat of summer rolled down my face. Silence like I had never heard or felt before embraced me. I stood in that door way allowing my eyes to adjust to the interior of this grand old abode. The smell of winter's damage and rain's many assaults became stronger as the house itself began to breathe outwardly. Broken windows, old raggedy furniture and wall paper long yellowed and stained by age created the stage for what was to be my first encounter with a truly "haunted" house.

I stepped inside to the crunching sound of broken glass beneath my feet and the smell of a house now mildewed and rotting. The atmosphere was heavy. I walked in a few more feet towards what seemed to have been a kitchen near the stairway leading to the upper part of the house. I stood a moment and then felt dread and decided to leave. As I turned to go I was once again aware of the whimpers of what I was sure was a puppy.

"Here boy...Here puppy!" I called out hoping to get it to come to me.

The sound continued and seemed to be coming from upstairs, so I mustered up my courage as I began walking up step by step. As I neared the upper landing I felt the presence of a spirit. I called out to it in anticipation of finding that perhaps another living soul had heard the dog as well and been upstairs looking for it.

"Is anyone up here? I think there is a hurt puppy up here. Is someone here?"

Despite hearing what sounded like footsteps, my calls were unanswered. I looked briefly into the nearest room whose door was gone. It contained an old bedroom set.

There were curtains blowing in the hot breeze tapping against the remains of the window pane.

I turned and began walking to another room when I heard the puppy whining at the farthest end of that dark and foreboding hallway. I felt that there was at least one other soul in that house. As I made my way to the end of the hall I glanced quickly into any open doorway and noticed it was becoming darker as though a storm was brewing outside.

Suddenly, the whimpering stopped! I heard what sounded like someone in the last room talking softly in a deep voice. I picked up the leg of a broken chair in fear that someone might be trying to trick me and attack me.

My intuition told me to leave but my youthful curiosity got the best of me. I opened the door and immediately saw a dark figure in the corner. I didn't wait to see who it was. I turned and ran down the hallway towards the stairs. Each step seemed an eternity! As I finally reached the landing, I stopped and turned to look, but quickly continued on when I heard the heavy footsteps behind me. As I bounded down the steps and out the door I turned long enough to see a short dark figure in the shadows at the foot of the steps.

As I ran away from the door, I heard a whispered voice say, "Pariah."

I jumped the fence, hopped on my bike, and didn't stop until I reached my house. I was both scared and awed by what had happened. I knew no one would believe me because I had not been believed when I told of my other encounters. I knew though that I had witnessed something otherworldly. I also knew that the energy was familiar...I had that same sense of not being afraid but knowing to keep my guard up all the same.

It was this event. This moment in my life that would set the tone for what was to come. I believed in ghost. I had seen an entity that both scared me and fascinated me. I couldn't wait to find another haunted house!

CHAPTER EIGHT:

The Ela Road Ghost

I was sixteen when a group of friends and I decided to try and find the Ela Road Ghost in Palatine, Illinois. Every town seems to have its hitchhiking ghost story and Palatine was no exception. The countless stories of the old man dressed in white with the long flowing beard and old style dress were as plentiful as stories of hidden marijuana plants in the middle of the corn fields. You always heard the stories on Monday of the haunted exploits of drunken friends parking near the Cade Cemetery in wait of the ghostly hitchhiker. It almost seemed to be a rite of passage for teenagers in the area.

We all met at my girlfriend's house in Hoffman Estates so we could caravan in two cars to Cade Cemetery. Being the good kids we were, we made sure we were fully prepared for what was ahead of us.

"I have a bottle of Jack to help us stay warm." A bottle of Jack Daniels was always necessary at any gathering in those days. My girlfriend was in charge of the beverages.

"Cigarettes and junk food, here!" Danny never hesitated to fill in the other vices.

"Okay, Jen and I can take two other people in my car." I drove my '65 Mustang and my friend drove his parents' Ford station wagon.

The drive there was small talk and silly dares to be fulfilled when we arrived at the cemetery. When we got there we parked in the driveway of the old worn down mansion nearby. It was somewhat reminiscent of the old southern antebellum homes.

"Do you smell that? I think it's roses," I said as we all got out of the autos. The smell of roses was unusual for an October filled with autumn's decay.

"Wow, that's pretty sweet smelling. It's actually kind of a sickening sweet." Jen was more of a Love's Lemon Soft kind of girl.

One of our group said we should lock the cars because he thought he saw someone near the back of the mansion's property. I looked in that direction and saw what appeared to be a person in the shadows of the tree line. At first I thought it was the creature from the shadows that seemed to call itself Pariah. After a moment though I didn't feel anything to worry about so we set out for the cemetery hoping to see the old man in white.

The cemetery was an older one. There were several stones knocked over, cracked and deteriorated from age and poor materials. Old tall trees seemed to stand amidst the graves like sentries standing guard over the few souls that had chosen to remain near this sanctified ground.

As teenagers will do, we got bored quickly and began to play graveyard tag and other silly games until we each found some secluded section of the graveyard to make out in. (The odd things we think are okay as teenagers become questionable as we age.)

As the midnight hour loomed near we all returned to the gates of the cemetery. It was there that a member of our group began to make it clear he was angry at us.

"Who kept throwing the pine cones at us? It wasn't funny, assholes!" Dannie was seriously mad as the interruptions had kept him from accomplishing his goal of having sex in the cemetery. He apparently got it in his head that we were messing with him.

"Dude, we were all too busy to mess with you!" Debbie made it clear she thought he was being silly. "You are just a wuss!"

We assured him that we had not done anything to ruin his moment. Some suggested it was probably just squirrels gathering food for the winter. Then, before we could say another word, we saw a shadowy figure standing by one of the graves located in the dark shade of a tall oak tree. There was a greenish glow around it, and it seemed to float just a few inches above the ground.

Being typical teenagers we looked at each other, and then, we ran.

As we got to our cars and locked ourselves in we were blasted by a green light. It lasted a moment and then disappeared. As I pulled out I noticed a shadowy figure at the door of the dilapidated mansion as well as a woman dressed in white on the balcony above. The beeping car horn of my friend who could not back out until I did forced my attention to backing out and leaving. I knew I had to go back though. I knew there was more to the Ela Road Ghost than most knew.

As we sped away like frightened children we drove by what appeared to be an old man dressed in white with a long beard. None of us would double back to see if we had actually seen him. We started talking on the way back and compared what we had seen. We could not wait to get back to school on Monday!!!

CHAPTER NINE:

The Ela Road Mansion Ghosts

A few weeks had passed and Halloween was just a few days away, so my girlfriend and I decided to return to Ela Road to check out the old mansion. She had smelled the roses and seen what she thought was the woman in white on the second floor. She knew about my gifts, and it often fascinated her when I would relate the things I saw and sensed. This was her chance to have a real haunting experience firsthand.

"I can't wait! I hope we see lots of ghosts!!!" Jen was excited to head out.

"Well, we may not find a thing. Maybe they won't even show themselves. Maybe they don't like tall blondes..." I loved to kid with her and she knew it.

"Hmmm. Maybe they don't like smartass skinny boys!" She smiled and snuggled close to me as we began our drive to Ela Road.

We arrived at the mansion shortly before dusk. It was warm for an autumn night and we were filled with energy!

As we drove up the driveway I decided to turn the car around in the event we might need to leave quickly.

As we stood in front of the old house so I could get my bearings, we both noticed the strong smell of roses.

"There's that rose smell again!" We spoke quickly and simultaneously.

When we approached the front door we noticed two rose vines climbing up the façade of the house and spreading wildly about. There were no roses on the decaying vines but it seemed as though the smell of roses was everywhere.

It didn't take much to open the door and walk into the wide entry parlor of the ruins. It looked as though someone had just walked out of the place and left everything behind. Old chairs, mirrors and various sticks of furniture dotted the room. There was an immense winding stairway that seemed to lead up forever into the darkness of the upper floor.

"Which way do we go?" Jen asked.

"Well, since we saw the woman in white upstairs I guess we should head that way." We walked forward into what seemed to be an ante room and sat a moment on an old over stuffed couch. As we sat there listening to our own breathing the room seemed to light up with a soft green energy, almost as though illuminated by fireflies on a summer night. There was a breeze from the upper level that seemed to whisper in the hallways. After a few moments we decided to walk upstairs.

The stairway seemed as though it were made of marble and had coldness to it that we could feel through our shoes. Each step we took seemed almost mystical in that we seemed to float up the stairs rather than climb. As we neared the top, we both were startled by what appeared to be a woman in white exiting the hall into a room down the way.

We stood still for a moment until Jen spoke. "Oh my god! Did you see that?"

"I think so. She went down the hall." Even though I had become used to seeing spirits it always through me off a little when I came across a full body apparition.

We cautiously approached the entry to the hallway. As we reached the door, we heard what sounded like a woman crying. We opened the door slowly and were surprised to find a room that was fully furnished and looked as though it was being lived in. The woman was sitting at a vanity leaning over sobbing as though she had lost everything. As we approached her she stood with her back to us and began to speak.

"I had planned to marry a gentleman long ago. I was from an affluent family, and my father did not hesitate to spoil me. There was a problem though. As a child I had been in a fire and my face was scarred." She cast aside her veil to show that her face had been partially ravaged by the fire. "I rarely had visitors except for tutors and, as such, my father worried for my future."

We stood there frozen in place and speechless.

"In my nineteenth year an older gentleman found his way to the mansion and offered to tutor me in the sciences. It wasn't long before I had fallen madly in love with this older gentleman and we were soon engaged to be married." A beautiful soft smile fell across her face.

"Father would spare no expense and began to plan the wedding. As a gift he was signing over half of his fortune to my fiancé and me. My beau convinced me to ask my father to do this early so we could buy a home and be able to settle down immediately." Her soft smile gave way to a sad somberness.

She explained that the wedding day came; and as the guests arrived for the joyous occasion it became evident that someone was missing.

"As the wedding hour approached father grew suspicious and went to his office to find that my betrothed had taken the promised moneys and ran away. Father returned to the mansion to gather a group of men to find the cur and punish him. For me... it was too much to bear." She looked at us with regret and sadness then vanished before our eyes.

I looked at Jen; she was crying. We stood for a moment and then returned to the hallway.

As we started to descend the stairwell my girlfriend screamed in surprise! I looked to our right and there in the shadows was a figure in black... the same figure we had seen on the grounds of the mansion and at the door a few weeks earlier.

He stood there for a moment and then he spoke...

"I am Corrine's Father. Before I left to run down the con man that had hurt my daughter so, I wanted to tell her I loved her. As I walked into my daughter's room I was met with tragedy. She had taken poison and lay dead surrounded by the flowers from her bridal bouquet...Roses."

Jen and I looked at each other but remained silent.

"Infuriated, my men and I searched frantically for the scoundrel who had caused such a thing. Shortly we found a body near the swamp a mile down the road by the far side of the cemetery. The body had been mangled nearly beyond recognition. His formal white attire was covered in blood and grease and looked as though he had been hoping to hitchhike into the darkness. By his body we found small foot prints and a single rose."

The father told us he had returned to his daughter's room to grieve her death. As he stood above her lifeless body lying in the bed, he noticed she had something clutched in her hand... a red carnation. Her lecherous groom had been wearing such a flower. Then the father was shocked by one more observation...the bride was barefoot and her feet were covered in mud as though she had left the house.

He began to cry and slowly made his way to the room where his daughter had died. As he opened the door he softly vanished.

"What a sad story. How horrible. Can't you do something to help them?" Jen was crying uncontrollably.

"I think that by listening to their stories and allowing them to finally meet in one place we may have helped them. I think they know it's ok to go to the beyond now." I wasn't sure but felt that they had found some peace.

We walked down the stairs and made our way to the door. The smell of roses was no longer lingering in the air. The old house felt different. It simply seemed to not have a feeling at all.

We got to my car and locked ourselves inside. As I tried to get a sense of what had happened, we sat a moment as the sun vanished behind the late night autumn clouds.

There was a silence that seemed familiar to me. Suddenly we noticed the dark figure just under the tree nearest my car. I drove out of the drive and, as my headlights shined briefly on the house, we saw roses on the rose vines. I didn't stop as we sped down the road.

Jen would never again do a walk through with me. The experience had been too much for her. She would talk about that night on Ela Road for a while, and then completely stopped mentioning it or talking about it. Over the years we would visit haunted sites because she still wanted very much to share my life. We would eventually marry after I went on to college and then into the military.

CHAPTER TEN:

The Shadow Creature Follows Me

It seemed that as I got older I encountered the shadow creature more frequently. When I was 18 my sister and I were returning from the store. We turned onto Western Street in Hoffman Estates and had just passed Flagstaff Blvd when we saw him.

"Oh, my god. Look at that creepy little man over there!" My sister was totally freaked out. "Don't stop! Let's get home. Rod, he's really scary!"

He was standing on the corner…no…he was somewhat floating. As we neared him he turned slowly and stared at us with his black glaring eyes and aged face. His pasty white albino skin was wrinkled and blemished giving him a haggardly expression. His skin seemed to almost shift like wax melting in the heat of a summer night. He tipped his hat at us and flashed a dark smile as we drove by as though he knew what we could never fathom. He watched as we pulled into our driveway two doors down and seemed to slowly drift our way.

"Get into the house." I stood guard as my sister made her way into the house and then I ran in behind her. "Quick, lock the door!"

We closed the drapes to keep him from looking into the house. We eventually found the courage to peek out only to find him standing at the bottom of the driveway... glaring at us. His overcoat and cape seemed to have a life of their own as they moved methodically in the slight wind.

We called the police. Then each of us found something to use as a weapon.

It seemed like an eternity before the police arrived, and in spite of the fact that we had monitored the dark spirit's movements, he had vanished when they came into view. His black piercing stare and aged face were burned into my brain. That blackness which seemed to be even darker than the shadow's yet darkly lit as though by some arcane ebony aura was all too familiar to me. I knew then that we would eventually have a spiritual confrontation. It was as though he was waiting for me to grow older, wiser and stronger.

CHAPTER ELEVEN:

Rosewood Massacre

In the spring of 1977, while at a Baptist College, I was sitting around with friends at a fast food place called Mr. Fish in Lakeland, Florida. We had finished classes for the day and as usual ended up here for soda and fries. It was a typically warm spring day and as always we found ourselves floating from one conversation to another. One of the ladies named Crystal somehow got us on the subject of haunted places.

"I was raised in a small town in Illinois along the Mississippi River called Nauvoo. We were one of the few families in town that were not Mormons. Our house was pretty old and had been built by Joseph Smith the Founder of the church. We had lived there about three months when the ghost visited us." Her voice had lowered to a loud whisper.

"I woke up around 3 a.m. There was the sound of someone walking up and down the hallway in boots. I got up to peek out into the hallway but didn't see anyone. I noticed my sister had also been trying to see who was up and about, so I darted over to her door and snuck quickly inside. Neither of us had seen a thing. I slept in her room for the rest of the night." She admitted they had put a chair against the locked door as a precaution.

"The next morning, we woke up and ran downstairs to see if anyone else had the same experience. No one else seemed to have noticed anything. This went on for a few weeks until one night when we all were awakened by a loud screaming man's voice... "Get out! Leave this house! They are coming for you!"...He was insistent, and we all ran to the front door. It was my father who made us come to our senses. He said we had all let our imaginations get to us and to go back to bed. I found out later that he didn't sleep a wink and had watched over us all night." She looked at each of us as she spoke.

"For the most part, we endured these visits until one spring a few years ago when a tornado tore through the town and destroyed the house. We had already learned that the house had belonged to a man who was supposed to be Joseph Smith's bodyguard, but apparently he had failed to protect the church leader and some members were seeking to put him on trial. A loyal friend had come to warn him but was accidently killed during the ensuing events." She seemed proud that she had been able to do such research.

"After the tornado, the house was rebuilt and we never had a problem again." With that statement she ended her story.

(Years later I visited Nauvoo but was not able to verify her story historically.)

A few others told their versions of local ghost stories which were more urban myth than anything. Finally, after a myriad of "true" ghost stories we fell upon the story of a small shanty town in Florida named Rosewood.

Rosewood had a history of violence. There were many claims that a visit to the remains of the town would always produce supernatural happenings. Since we were all from other states, we had no real knowledge of Rosewood's true history; back in those days you couldn't just Google information. All we knew was that it was indeed a haunted spot and we were bored college students!

"We have a four day weekend coming up! I think we should visit Rosewood and then go to the Gulf of Mexico for the rest of the weekend. The beaches are great this time of year." Chuck was the first to suggest such a trip, and before we knew it we had decided it would be perfect for our upcoming weekend.

"I think we all need to chip in equally for gas and rooms." I felt that should be made clear as I had been taken advantage of before on such trips and ended up paying more than my share.

"Everyone needs to chip in on food and pop as well." Crystal seemed to feel the same way I did about such trips.

By Friday morning we had all gathered our things and were anxious to head out on our adventure. We set out for Rosewood but ended up in a town further down the way called Cedar Keys. We finally found lodging and stayed at a motel that seemed right out of the movie *Psycho*. I can only hope that it has long since given way to a finer establishment or an opportune fire.

There were ten rooms available under the very judgmental eye of the owner. After a fifteen minute lecture on the evils of promiscuity, we were given the keys to four rooms, two for the boys and two for the girls... on opposite sides of the building.

We spent the rest of the day and evening in Cedar Key enjoying a nice café and the local beach. As you can imagine, we were constantly under the eye of locals somewhat suspicious of young folks who would come to this particular location instead of other more youth oriented places. We decided not to say we were there to visit the local haunted spot and instead said we were just trying to get away from the crowds.

During breakfast the next morning, Crystal decided to ask for directions to Rosewood.

The waitress got real quiet. "What in blazes do you want to go see that old place for? Ain't nobody even live there no more 'ceptin a few hangers on."

"We were just curious and thought since it was on our way we would check it out." Crystal was polite and made sure to add a touch of naiveté to her voice.

"You need to hush up about that old ruin and go home!" The waitress gave us a stern warning. She then went back to her counter area and began telling everyone she could about us.

An older gentleman got up and came over. He told us we needed to mind our own business and let things be. At this point we were all fairly confused about why there was such a reaction to our wanting to have a little fun in a ghost town.

The waitress brought our bill and pretty much ignored us after that. I sensed a lot of anger towards us and persuaded everyone to head back to the motel. When we got there the owner walked briskly up to us and said that he didn't want any trouble and that we needed to leave! He had already sent the maid, an African American woman, to clean our rooms. (Amazing what people could get away with 40 years ago!)

We were stunned. This motel was affordable for us, and we had planned to stay there when we went to the gulf to swim. We walked back to our rooms where we ran into the maid who was busy cleaning them. I took a chance and asked her about Rosewood. She laughed, and then looked around for a moment to be sure she was free to talk.

"My name is Brenda," she offered. "A long time ago, Rosewood had been a town filled by African Americans. Then around 1920 it was wiped out by people from local towns." She said.

"I heard that there had been a white woman who claimed she was assaulted by a black man, and the white townsfolk attacked the town. When they had finished only one building remained, and it was owned by a white man named Wight." She thought that was pretty funny.

She warned us to not ask much more about it but did let us know if we went up Highway 24 we would pass right by it. We packed our things, paid for our rooms, and headed to another motel in another town by way of Rosewood.

We ended up going back and forth a couple of times before we found what remained of Rosewood. The site was mostly overgrown and there was what I seem to remember as a town marker of sorts. We pulled off the road into what seemed more of a long driveway than a road. In the distance was a beautiful old house typical of the south during the early 1900s. There was an older man out mowing the lawn who informed us he was the caretaker for the family that owned the property at the time.

The "town" was dark and angry feeling. Old trees that I sensed had been used as lynching spots stood solemn and cold. The air smelled of long ago deaths, and the ground seemed hard and bitter. The feel of death was the strongest I had ever felt.

Suddenly, I began to feel souls gathering near us as though they were curious to see these silly children seeking ghosts. I told my friends that they were there, and of course, I was met with disbelief. I decided to walk off by myself toward the old house.

I stopped by what at one time was an old springhouse. It was a type of well that supplied folks in the town with fresh spring water. The well seemed to hold fear deeper than the water within it. Children had been hidden in this well in freezing water for hours in an attempt to avoid the horrible beatings and lynching. If you listened you could hear the stifled cries and sense the fear laden tears of these children. It was here that I came in contact with the old woman who seemed to be standing guard over the well.

"I know you can see me. I have been watching you since you came here." She was an older African American dressed in clothing that was "fashionable" to her people in the 1920's. "I would think you see enough spirits without looking for more."

"I guess I am just curious about it." I immediately felt like that was a silly response.

"What a silly thing to say. The spirits here have long since found peace, and those that remain try to keep life here as it was before the dark time." She almost seemed to be telling me I was stirring up bad energy and not welcome. "You sense the truth so listen to it and leave!"

I had forgotten that when I connect to spirits it is sometimes a mutual connection and thoughts become transparent to each of us. I apologized, wished her well and walked away.

I approached the man mowing the lawn and asked about the building that remained.

He introduced himself as a defendant of the owner. "During the massacre the house belonged to my great uncle, a business man named Wight. He tried to help many of the families escape the wrongful retribution of the local townsfolk bent on avenging a crime that did not happen."

The building itself was the only light I felt on the entire property. Many families had been allowed to hide in the groves near there to wait out the attack. I felt as though not only Mr. Wight but several entities were present in that grand home watching over it and perhaps still watching over souls of those who still had not been able to break away from that time of horror.

I had realized that some of those townspeople in Cedar Key had been alive during this time or had family members involved in this horrible event. I am told that a marker is there now and that Mr. Wight's home and property still remain in good condition.

CHAPTER TWELVE:

Grandma's Story

While in Florida I spent time with my Grandma. My mom's side of the family lived in or near Wahneta. I saw this as an opportunity to talk to Grandma about all the stories I had heard as a child. Grandma loved to talk about the old days, and I learned that the stories of my youth were indeed true. I was surprised, however, to find out that Grandma's mother had been intuitive as well.

"Momma was a righteous woman and followed the Lord's word. She always turned to the Bible if things worried her and always found answers." Grandma spoke almost as if she were back in her youth. "She knew things and had knowledge that even she couldn't say where it came from. She just said that God had seen fit to give her that knowledge to use to help folks."

I was in awe that my gift may have come from my great grandmother. As grandma talked, I saw similarities between my gift and the things my great grandma had done. Could it be that in some way I had inherited this gift?

The one thing that stood out most about great grandma was that she had the ability to see someone's sickness and even to know when they had died. The older I got the more this part of the gift became noticeable and the more I began referring to this part of my gift as a curse.

Grandma and I talked about this for a while. The more I learned the more I came to accept this gift for what it was. I began to see things less in black and white and more in the diverse way my gift worked. I began to understand that I had more control of it than I thought, and that eventually it would take me to a life choice I would not have ever thought I would make.

CHAPTER THIRTEEN:

Chicago

I returned to Illinois after my stay in Florida and lived in a small apartment with my fiancé, Jen, in Arlington Heights, Illinois. I only had a few months until I was to be sent to a church in Louisiana to act as an assistant pastor, so Jen and I decided to spend some time exploring Chicago. We had gotten interested in the emerging Disco scene and found ourselves frequenting many of the Discotheques and dance clubs in downtown Chicago along Rush and Clark streets. It was a great time until the drug culture began to sweep through the discos and we found ourselves having fewer choices of clubs.

On one occasion some of us decided that rather than go clubbing we would visit the various haunted spots in Chicago. There were so many to choose from. Chicago has a history of fires, gangsters and serial killers. It has suffered through disease, Indian wars and riots. Even though many of the older more historic hotels and buildings are long gone the sites still seem to retain ghosts from days and events long past. Chicago is truly a mecca for ghost hunters.

We decided to go for the most famous site we knew at the time and drove to 2122 North Clark Street which is the site of what has become known as The Saint Valentine's Day Massacre. We found a nicely landscaped parking lot where the old warehouse once stood. Legend has it that you can hear gunshots and men pleading at different times. We parked for about an hour and even though we didn't hear anything the feel of this spot was horrendous. It bothered me that this historic site was now the parking lot next door to a nursing home.

"Okay, so it's a beat up wall and a parking lot?" Jen was not impressed; her eyes were just looking at a site.

"I heard a section of the wall where they were shot got sold off and some people stole bricks from the site, so I guess this is what's left." I was fairly disappointed myself.

"I hear all the cars and what sounds like gunshots though..." Danny wanted badly to find something here.

"Well, it is near a busy road and the gunshots are probably cars backfiring." I hated to rain on his parade but I had decided long ago to only accept real evidence and try to explain everything else.

Since we didn't feel anything unusual there, we decided to drive down to the Biograph Theater to see if we could spot the ghost of John Dillinger. We parked down from 2433 North Lincoln Avenue and walked the two blocks to the theater. As we approached it, we came to an alley. For a moment, I grew dizzy and disoriented.

Danny mentioned, "That's the alley I heard Dillinger stumbled into after he'd been shot by FBI agents."

I stood there a moment looking at a figure laying in the dark alley with three men standing over him. I felt that this was indeed Dillinger and described the scene only I could see to my friends.

"There is a man lying in the alley with blood all over him. He isn't moving. There are three men standing over him with guns. One of them said, 'So long, Johnny.' Another keeps saying, 'We need to take a picture when the director gets here.' I think they are waiting for J. Edgar Hoover!"

"No freaking way! How do you do that?" Craig was obsessed by the supernatural, and I am sure would have given anything to have my gift. Most people seem to feel that way until they witness the downsides of it.

"I'm starved. Let's grab something to eat." Jen always knew when to change the subject for me and help me avoid long drawn out explanations and stories.

We had dinner at a local diner and shared our adventure with the waitress.

She asked, "Did you see the lady in red people claim to see standing at the front door of the Biograph? She's the one who set up Dillinger for the F.B.I."

"We were so busy looking in the alley that we didn't notice anything else." I was mad at myself for not taking time to look around.

After dinner we walked by the Biograph again to see if by chance we might spot the ghostly image of Dillinger's alleged betrayer. When we had no luck, we decided to visit one last site.

We drove to 2428 West Randolph Street to investigate another alley. On December 30, 1903, the Iroquois Theatre caught fire. This theater had been advertised as the grandest theatre ever and fireproof as well. During a performance by Eddie Foy, a famous actor in those days, a fire curtain tragically caught fire and 602 lives were lost.

The audience was mostly women and children as there had been no school. At first Foy joked with the audience about the flames because he assumed the asbestos fire curtains would do their job. Shortly into his act, he realized the flames were more than incidental and told the audience to slowly exit the theater. Then he left the stage. Foy and the entire cast and crew of his show managed to escape unharmed.

Foy's reputation suffered a bit because people thought at first he had been responsible for misleading the audience into staying until it was too late. Foy would carry that grief with him for the rest of his life.

The fire was massive and quick. The very measures taken to insure that the theatre was fireproof had instead turned it into a blazing oven whose inferno was so hot that bodies were melted together. After the fire, bodies were laid in the alley behind the remains of the theater for loved ones to attempt to identify. To this day people claim to hear cries of woman and children coming from the alley.

The theatre building's shell survived the fire, and its outer walls became part of the Colonial Theatre which was built on the same spot soon after. The Colonial was demolished years later, replaced by the Oriental Theatre. Over the years the alley was left alone until public resurgence in Chicago ghost folklore brought it back to life.

We stood there staring, a little hesitant to go into the poorly lit alley. The theatre district in Chicago has always been somewhat odd and knowing that this tragedy occurred in the heart of the district gave it an even more mystical appeal. I caught my breath and began to zone so I could get a sense of what might be there.

"Did you get anything yet? What do you see?" Danny was like a kid at Christmas.

"Give him a minute," said Jen, always my protector.

I stepped into the alley and immediately felt the fear and terror of all those children knowing they were going to die.

"Mommy! Help Me!" "It hurts!" "Where is my baby?" Screams of the long dead souls echoed out of the alley.

I had never felt such terror before! Suddenly, I realized I was crying. It was horrible! There were bodies lying everywhere and souls roaming around as though searching for lost ones. (Some bodies were never truly identified.)

"I didn't know. I thought it was ok. They told me it would be okay and to get my children to safety." The voice came from the direction of the stage door. I saw a guilt-ridden man standing there filled with sorrow and realized it was Eddie Foy. Clearly he had carried to his grave some sense of not doing enough during the tragedy.

He was attempting to gather the ghosts of the children, perhaps in hopes of delivering them to their beyond. For a moment he looked at me as though asking for some unnecessary absolution. He had done nothing out of spite or ill intent. He stays, I believe, in hopes of helping each of these souls reach Heaven.

I couldn't stay in the alley long and finally had to leave. Pain, suffering and fear inundated that alley. There had been too many lives lost and too many souls wandering aimlessly for me to deal with.

This was truly the greatest fire tragedy in American History, and it could have been avoided had the owners not taken short cuts. I stood on the sidewalk looking at the scene, wishing I could do more, but knowing that these souls had to find their own ways for different reasons. Instead, I simply offered a prayer for peace and rest. Years later, I returned to that alley and found that most of the spirits had indeed gone on. Eddie Foy was still there and still watching over them.

CHAPTER FOURTEEN:

An Old Friend

I knew shortly after arriving at the church I'd been
assigned to that I had made a mistake. I had known since
the age of nine that I would have a ministry, but this was
not the right time. Jen and I had broken up the year before,
and I was still very upset. I wanted to stay in Illinois but
knew I had a legal obligation to this church for two years.
So here I was, preaching in a little town about an hour
away from Fort Polk, Louisiana.

On one Sunday after services, I found my way down the
road to a long established Black Gospel church that I had
driven by on a few occasions but never stopped in. This
particular Sunday I seemed to be drawn to this church. I
walked in just as services were beginning, but instead of
continuing on, the minister stopped to greet me.

"Welcome, Friend! We are glad you could join us!" He
wasn't much older than I was but had a lot more
confidence in his voice. "Ladies and gentleman, join me in
welcoming this gentleman."

The congregation turned my way, and I was flooded with wonderfully warm salutations.

"Thank you. My name is...." but before I could finish I was interrupted by the voice of a human angel.

"Rodney...and he loves lemonade and cookies." I turned toward that voice and saw a most beautiful woman! Instantly I knew it was Adrienne Dimanche, the young girl who had greeted my grandmother and me years ago. She walked over and motioned for me to follow her toward a seat in the front. We sat down quietly together as the minister began his sermon.

As I sat there I did my best to not stare at Adrienne but her aura was glowing brightly and beautifully. I felt as though all time had stopped and we had never parted ways. Here we were a thousand miles and more than a decade away from when we had last met and it was as though had not missed a moment of time together.

The church service was alive with "Amens" ad "Hallelujahs!" This congregation was filled with the spirit and proud of it. Hymns were sung and testimonies given before the final prayer. Afterwards, there would be a fine pot luck picnic, perfect for socializing and getting reacquainted!

Adrienne and I had a lot to talk about! I knew that she had stayed with her mother as long as possible but eventually had to go live with her grandma. She went to school for art and library science.

"I have never forgotten you. The first time I saw you, I was totally breathless. I guess that's a little silly." I wasn't sure how she would take that bit of information.

"I know. I also knew we would meet again. There was just something special that made me feel like we were connected." She smiled and gave me a warm hug.

"You know your mother was right about me and my life, right? It has not been normal at all. I just wish it had been easier." I felt so comfortable talking to her, a far cry from when we were younger.

"Well, I figured it wouldn't be boring for you." She smiled and changed the subject.

"Can I ask you a question?" I didn't wait for her permission and continued to talk. "Your mother's last name was 'Sunday' but your last name was 'Dimanche'; why is that?"

"'Dimanche' is french for 'Sunday'. Your mind is so marvelous; so peculiar in the way it seems to grab at such odd things." She giggled a little and changed the subject.

We talked most of the day and ended up sitting on the porch of her grandma's house. We talked about her mom a bit and my grandma. I told her about some of my adventures with spirits and expected her to run into the house and lock the door. Instead she listened and made it clear that she not only wanted to be a part of my life but also had an odd hobby... she liked to visit haunted houses!

CHAPTER FIFTEEN:

The Myrtles Plantation

Thanks to Adrienne's familiarity with the area, I had the opportunity to walk through many "haunted" sites. On three occasions I stayed at the antebellum style manor called the Myrtles Plantation in St. Francisville, Louisiana near Baton Rouge. Legend has it that this manor was built upon an ancient Indian burial ground.

The plantation's history is a little clouded, a blend between local truth and haunted fiction. Rumors of events ranging from murder to molestation and the raping of slaves are accompanied by claims of angry spirits of former owners, murder victims, and southern soldiers. Stories of dark shadow creatures, faces in the mirrors, and whispers in the air are as frequent as ghost sightings of one or two of the owners, a woman in white, and various wisps of smoke.

In 1981, I was invited by Adrienne to spend the weekend with her and her family. Adrienne was Creole Cajun from Baton Rouge and her family had been connected to the plantation through her grandmother who had been born a slave but was freed on the plantation. Many of the freed slaves chose to remain on the plantation to work as sharecroppers or household help. Adrienne's grandmother was kept on as a maid and allowed to live on the grounds of what at that time was a grand plantation. The Myrtles property has since been sold off to various folks; now what remains is a bed and breakfast sitting on around ten acres.

Adrienne and I reserved a beautiful room reminiscent of the New Orleans antebellum days. We arrived shortly before dinner on Friday and decided to join the rest of the guest in the main dining area. It was a quaint and cozy little room with several tables. I am told it has since been enlarged to accommodate more guests. We sat there enjoying polite conversation and good southern cooking until it was time to retire to the parlor for dessert and coffee.

We sat by the fireplace and enjoyed the warmth of the grand old hearth. As we relaxed there, we began to hear a very faint sound of music that seemed to be floating on the soft summer wind amongst the old tall trees.

"Do you hear that?" Adrienne had not yet learned of my gift.

"It sounds like a band playing softly in the bayou." I knew it was other worldly but figured I would wait to see her reaction.

"It's so beautiful, and it seems familiar even though I don't remember ever hearing it." Adrienne seemed almost distant in her thoughts.

Suddenly, Adrienne stood up and walked to the window. "Rod, there's a young woman standing at the window. I swear she's dressed like it was a hundred years ago."

"I swear I saw a young black woman stop a moment and disappear into the night." She turned to me with a look of confusion.

"Maybe it's someone they pay to play the part of a woman from the Civil War era to entertain guests." I knew better but had to offer up something.

I had already sensed that this young woman had been visiting this home for some time. In death, she was now continuing her visit searching for someone who I perceived was a long lost lover.

We finished our dessert of red velvet cake and chicory coffee, then took a walk amongst the trees in the warm Louisiana night. There was a smell of lavender in the air that seemed out of place.

"It's odd, but I feel like I have been here before; that I have lived on this plantation." I had never had such a strong sense of déjà vu in my life!

"Honestly? That's so weird because I've felt like I belong here too." Adrienne was not one to agree with me unless she truly felt something.

I began sensing spirits around us in a way never experienced before. I felt as though they could reach within me and guide me through the grounds and the house. I decided I needed to go inside and was about to say so when Adrienne mentioned she was ready to go to our room.

The room was decorated in antebellum style wallpaper with a large bed and overstuffed furniture. Moonlight streamed through the large windows bathing us in its glow. A large ceiling fan seemed to be singing us to sleep. We talked a bit and then gave in to the fan's lullaby and fell asleep.

Around 2 a.m., Adrienne woke me up. Our room was filled with a blue iridescent glow. I remember briefly wondering if we'd gone back in time. Then I felt a spirit trying to communicate with me and saw that Adrienne was experiencing something similar as well. Concrete thoughts faded out as physical sensing expanded and expanded, enveloping us together in a passion never ever felt before. It was like strong energy surging into our mutual libidos charging us into a passionate embrace.

We felt like two lovers who had long ago been separated and now had reunited. There was a passion reawakened within each of us never experienced before in this lifetime. It seemed as through our bodies had been taken over by the spirits of two long separated lovers. Hours passed before we fell to sleep from exhaustion.

We awoke the next morning and lay there in silence; neither of us sure if the night's passion was real; neither of us brave enough to ask the other. Then we embraced, igniting the new sense of familiarity and body knowing. Finally, I calmly asked if she had experienced the same passionate event that I had. We both had tears in our eyes from the shared moment. We lay there quietly for some time and then arose for the day.

That afternoon we talked with Adrienne's grandmother. She told us a story her mother had relayed to her about how her mother had once fallen in love with the son of one of the owners and had an affair. When the owner found out, he sent the son away to college and forbade the young girl to ever come to the main house again. Adrienne and I learned that when the son returned, he would sneak the girl into his room. They remained lovers until he died at a young age. Adrienne's great-grandmother then met a fellow and married.

Our first stay at The Myrtles Plantation was an amazing event and one in which I believe we channeled and brought together two long ago lovers.

CHAPTER SIXTEEN:

The French Quarter Author

Located at the end of world famous Bourbon Street is a section of New Orleans called the French Quarter. Most of its buildings date back to the early 1800's. Its history is filled with mystery, magic and murder! I have been able to visit New Orleans on many occasions. It's a city with an almost mystical feel to it that radiates wonderful energy.

You have to understand something about the French Quarter to truly appreciate its many haunted locations. It sits along the Mississippi River just a short way from the Gulf of Mexico. When I visited that section of the city, I learned that the area along the river was called the Moon Walk, and the feeling arising from that spot was beyond mystical.

A short distance inland is Jackson Square with its small shops and artists surrounding the old St. Louis Cathedral. Legend has it that voodoo queens and monastic figures have long haunted this location. On some nights when the mists from the river flow softly inland through the streets and slither magically around the old buildings you are taken back in time to a place long dead but still filled with life.

My first official visit to the old city was in 1979 at the request of a friend of Adrienne's who was stationed at Fort Polk located near Leesville, Louisiana. This friend's brother was living with a budding young writer in what had been the former residence of author Tennessee Williams. It was actually more of an attic apartment located at 722 Toulouse Street in what is known as the Vieux Carre district. (I thought it was somewhat odd since Williams had often written that he wanted to die in his former residence at 1014 Dumaine Street.)

Williams had died just a few months prior, and they had been experiencing some very odd things.

The haunting began with the simple smell of coffee and cigarettes which Williams was known to use in massive quantities when he would write. However, it was known that neither current occupant was a smoker, and both preferred chicory coffee. Since chicory coffee has a very definite smell quite unlike the smotherless bitter smell we were all experiencing, it seemed likely the occupants were indeed experiencing a ghostly connection. They made the assumption that it was simply a smell drifting from another apartment as the old buildings had long since lost a degree of privacy along with the insulated sound proofing. Obviously, Adrienne had already talked to the tenants.

"It wasn't until they began to hear the tapping noises in the wee hours of the morning that they began to suspect that they had another other worldly roommate. At first they thought they had heard some loose shutter knocking against the outside of a window. After a few nights of this, the tapping began to develop a rhythm to it like someone typing," She continued. "Shortly afterwards they began to see a man in the shadows and hear a voice mumbling outside their entry or on their balcony. Once while cleaning up, they found a bottle of eyedrop liquid that did not belong there and heard sounds of a man choking."

The story was that Williams had choked to death in New York on the cap of an eyedrop bottle that he was known to use on a regular basis. (Years later it was proven that he had overdosed on the many drugs he was taking.)

"So, why are they asking me to check this stuff out?" I was very curious why they would even know me.

Adrienne flashed a wide smile at me. "Hello! They want you because you are a psychic medium like Jean Dixon!"

"You know? When did you figure it out?" I was totally blindsided.

"Mom knew you were, and then Grandma told me when I explained what happened at the Myrtles." Her eyes were wide and bright with wonderment.

"Wow, I was worrying about how to tell you or if I should even say anything!" I was so relieved that she knew, and she had stayed with me!!!

Adrienne introduced me to John and Gary who lived in the old place. We made a deal to stay at the apartment for two nights, and then we decided we would spend some time in the French Quarter.

Our stay in this old townhouse, which Williams had referred to as more of a garage apartment, was eventful. The first night I was awakened by typing sounds and the smell of cigarettes. Later in the night Adrienne heard footsteps and the soft mumbling of what seemed like a rant. When we awoke the next morning, all of our belongings were strewn all over the apartment as though someone had thrown them about in a mad search for drugs or such.

We walked around the neighborhood and spoke to some of the local artists and Bohemians about Williams and were directed to his home at 1014 Dumaine Street. Adrienne and I paused across the street for a few minutes to see what I might sense.

As we stood there, I saw a figure at the window appearing somewhat gaunt as though suffering from a lifelong ailment. The mustache and furrowed brow were unmistakably features of Tennessee Williams. I felt that he had indeed returned to his beloved Vieux Carre!

Adrienne and I returned to the tiny apartment knowing that it was indeed being visited by the author.

I explained to John and Gary, "You are indeed experiencing Williams, and he is harmless. He has simply returned to both your apartment and Vieux Carre, two places where he felt the most emotions in his life. I believe he is traveling back and forth and that you have experienced the fullest extent of this haunting. I suggest if you cannot live with your guest, you should contact either a minister or a local Priestess to cleanse the house and send Williams on his way."

"Oh, no! We are delighted to have him! This is so going to be a highlight of our next party!" Gary seemed genuinely thrilled.

I was happy that they felt honored to have Williams there and chose to allow him to stay. As we headed back to the train station to return home, we wandered a bit through the Quarter and decided to come back another time and see what I could find. We were not disappointed!

CHAPTER SEVENTEEN:

Jean Lafitte's Blacksmith Shop Pub

Adrienne had gotten a job with a lawyer in New Orleans and was living in a wonderful apartment in the French Quarter. I had finished my obligation to the little white church and decided to move in with Adrienne until I could figure out my next move. Adrienne's apartment was within walking distance of most places in the Quarter that we loved, including Jean Lafitte's Pub.

I visited this pub on almost every trip to New Orleans. It was one of the oldest remaining French architectural buildings in the Quarter that had not been refurbished on some level. It was a two story brick and stone building solidly built in the French style around the late 1700s. The great fires in 1788 and 1794 seemed to dance around this spot and leave it virtually untouched.

This building was owned by pirate Jean Lafitte and used as a black smith shop publicly while privately it served as a meeting place for spies and profiteers. The black smith shop operated on the first floor while other business was conducted on the second floor. Rumors of hidden stairwells and secret rooms have persisted for centuries.

For me, visiting the pub was like stepping back in time to the 18th Century. The pub's dark interior was accented by its authentic wood beamed ceiling and walls. It seemed dark because originally gaslights were used which barely offered any light, exactly what one would expect of such a place. The pub featured an old bar long worn from use, and the room was furnished with old wooden tables and chairs to match.

The first time I walked into the bar it took me several seconds to focus my eyesight in the darkly lit pub. We sat at the nearest table to avoid running into anything. As our eyes became accustomed to the dark, we felt more comfortable and moved farther into the room.

We ordered beer and chatted for a while until I could zone into the pub's energy. Then I shared my impressions with Adrienne.

"The first thing I seem to sense is a gentleman standing in the dark near the bar. He is tall with a medium build and a mustache that he seems to twist nervously. He is smoking a cigar and seems somewhat annoyed that I can see him."

We were now sitting near the fireplace. My focus on the gentleman lessened as I tuned into what seemed like eyes watching us. This sensation came from inside the fire grate as though eyes peered out from some hidden space.

"I feel as though some horrible event took place by this fireplace." Before I could continue...

"Oh. My lord! Someone just touched me. It was like ice!" Immediately, I could see that Adrienne was startled by this; it had really unnerved her.

She and another lady in attendance went to the ladies room to freshen up and to give Adrienne a chance to catch her breath. They returned abruptly claiming they had heard a man's voice coming from one of the stalls. The bartender immediately went to check it out but returned with the news it was probably one of the ghosts in the pub.

We finished our beers and were about to leave when I looked over to the stairwell and saw what I thought was a woman dressed in the New Orleans Style of the 1700's. She vanished before I could lock onto her so we decided to wait a little longer. The bartender, who had overheard our whole conversation, walked over to tell us that she could confirm most of what we had sensed.

This pub is one of my main stops in New Orleans because it is truly one of the remaining direct connections to its founding era. I am told that one reason it remains so close to its original condition is because the owners are able to work within building codes.

CHAPTER EIGHTEEN:

St. Louis Cathedral Basilica

The old cathedral located across the street from Jackson Square is one of the most haunted places in New Orleans. With a long history of religious worship and violence connected to this church, the energy surrounding it has drawn in many spirits. From long dead monks to voodoo queens, to victims of racial and ethnic violence, this place has many ghosts.

First of all, I highly recommend visiting Jackson Square and the Basilica because it's truly a wonderful place to visit. Quaint tourist shops and Voodoo shops surround the wonderful courtyard filled with artists and street entertainers. Spending some time watching the artists and sampling the food is part of the French Quarter tradition.

After you have enjoyed your day, I recommend taking a walk around the square in the evening hours. One particular day I had my girlfriend, Adrienne, with me. She had become a member of a local artist group in the area and was acting as my tour guide. Adrienne had a friend who could get us into places in the Basilica that were considered haunted so I could do a walk through. I was delighted when I realized that the hauntings were not just within the Basilica but all around Jackson Square.

We walked to the Square on a wonderfully warm but breezy day. The temperature and humidity were perfect, making it easier for me to concentrate on my mission. At first, I was overwhelmed by so many spirits present in that area.

We paused a few moments so I could zone. As I stood there letting myself open to the energies, I realized that Yeshua was with us but that he would only be there in spirit. This made me feel a bit safer as I began to sense many negative vibes.

"Wow, this is a really powerful place," I said to Adrienne. "The strongest energy I feel is a truly evil and cruel woman. She committed many unspeakable acts and has never been known to truly repent. I see her dressed in fine gowns and sense that she thinks of herself as some elite person." I noticed that a strong level of contempt for people seemed to radiate from her until she reached the Basilica. Then…she seemed to collapse in fear and pain as though seeking some absolution which she knew would never come.

After I described this woman to Adrienne, she told me, "This apparition is commonly seen here. People claim it is a woman named Madame LaLaurie.

"Madame LaLaurie was a socialite of the day with a somewhat clouded family history. She married a prominent wealthy gentleman with vast holdings, including slaves. Legend says that she was a cruel and abusive mistress to them. When a fire broke out in her home, the bodies of several slaves were found hidden in an attic room, all of them mutilated and skinned." Adrienne stopped a moment n sadness at such an act. "Word got out of the atrocities she had committed, and she was forced to flee to France. "

Madame LaLaurie was, for all intents and purposes, a possible serial killer!

As we continued our midnight troll, I felt the presence of six souls in front of the Basilica. At first, I thought they were bound to that location and couldn't leave.

"Why do you stay here? You are free to go." I had to know the answer.

We choose to stay to watch over the poor abused souls," one man answered quietly.

I also felt that they were choosing to stay as some symbolic challenge to a long dead master. The souls had been together in life and died a vicious death before their bodies were dumped in front of the church.

"Those six men were killed because of a miscommunication when the King of France gave

Louisiana to the Spanish. He neglected to tell his subjects of the change and when the Spanish rolled in and replaced the French flag with their own, these six men lead what they thought was a defense of their home from invaders." Adrienne had become my researcher at her own bequest. "The Spanish Governor took it as a brazen insult and had the men hunted down, killed, and had their bodies left in front of the church as a warning to others who might try to revolt. Their bodies were eventually stolen in the night and given a proper burial by the Monk in charge of the Basilica."

"Hmmm. Interestingly, I also feel the presence of the monk but only faintly. He says his name is Pere Dagobert. He is the monk who gathered a group to take the men's bodies and give them a proper burial." I listened as Pere talked, then relayed his message to Adrienne. "He says he made sure the graves were left unmarked and then escaped to another region. Pere's energy seems very loving, but I also sense strong determination as well."

"According to historical research he was well loved," Adrienne said, always attempting to confirm my readings.

We stopped to grab a hurricane drink and a bite to eat at one of the small eateries nearby. While sitting outside and enjoying the warm breeze, I noticed what appeared to be a beautiful woman with caramel skin and long hair dancing in front of the church on the square.

"Adrienne, there is a beautiful woman dancing in the courtyard. Her energy seems old and wise, yet almost sad with the sense she had been betrayed." I did not need my friend to tell me that this was Marie Laveau, the Voodoo Queen.

"Adrienne, this is kind of odd. I get a very contradictory energy from her as she spirals about in her colorful garments singing an old Creole spiritual. Her energy has the feel of Catholicism to it." This seemed totally contradictory to her more famous activities as a Voodoo Queen. An apparition that was both a follower of Christ and a practitioner of voodoo seemed absurd and unthinkable!

Adrienne suggested we visit Marie Laveau's voodoo shop to see what they thought. I had never been in an authentic voodoo shop! Most in the area were fake shops designed to sell trash and trinkets to tourist. As I walked in, I was overwhelmed by the energy.

Immediately the older woman at the counter came around and sprinkled me with holy water.

"You are one with night eyes and spirit vision!" She was excited and highly animated. "I am so happy that you saw my dear great grandmother as she truly was."

"What do you mean?" We had not said a word about anything that had happened.

"There are no secrets here." Her Creole Cajun accent was even heavier than Adrienne's. "The spirits tell everything."

She told us, "Marie Laveau was a devout Catholic who often helped the local priest in tending to the poor and the sick. She was a believer in Jesus Christ and adhered to the Bible as best she knew. She also followed voodoo and became the Local Priestess. This was somewhat accepted because of her countless selfless acts for the poor people of New Orleans. She was, however, denied a proper burial and was buried in an unmarked grave. A tomb was erected by her friends and followers."

We stayed and continued talking a bit. I asked about various things from potions to tinctures to blessings and more. Eventually, Adrienne pointed out that it was getting late and we had more sites to see. As we left the shop, the great granddaughter of Marie Laveau gave me a blessing.

She also warned me. "Know this. All things in the light of day are not good and all things in the darkest places are not bad. There is a balance to everything. Never assume you know the truth."

I thanked her, and we walked towards Adrienne's apartment a few blocks away. We arrived at 811 Royal Street around 11:00 p.m. and made our way upstairs to Adrienne's small loft of an apartment. I loved the old New

Orleans townhome apartments because each one has its own character.

The high ceilings and windows to match made me feel as though I had stepped back in time. The wide planked wooden floors, plastered walls, and built in shelves brought me back to older days. The bathroom was straight out of an old romance novel with its deep claw foot tub, pedestal sink, and cool tile floor.

I could feel both inspiration and desperation in these old buildings. A previous owner had left heavy energy, and I felt sorry for him. But I had no idea who the occupant was. Years later, I found out that this particular apartment not only had a tie to Tennessee Williams, it also had been a temporary home to Truman Capote, author of *Breakfast at Tiffany's* and *In Cold Blood.*

CHAPTER NINETEEN:

Mississippi River and Roaming Spirits

We awoke bright and early to enjoy the last day of my visit. The next morning I was heading out to visit a friend in Alexandria. Before I left, Adrienne had one last ghostly encounter she was hoping to share with me, but we had to wait until after sunset when the mist rolled in off the river into the French Quarter.

We began our day with breakfast biscuits and bitter chicory coffee. Then we decided to walk along the various streets and visit the shops. As it turned out, stopping to enjoy the corner artists and street musicians who dotted the Quarter was the perfect way to spend our time.

Adrienne was due to paint for a few hours in a spot she shared with two other artists, so I took advantage of this and walked along the river and down the various alleyways with hidden turns and dead ends.

While walking, I came upon a home that had been neglected; its yard over grown. This seemed a rare thing in this particular part of the Quarter. The building was a typical three story townhome with the large high windows and ornate outer façade. It was painted a dark olive green with black trim. The upper windows were covered by long shutters and the windows of the second floor were adorned with dark burgundy curtains that were opened enough to see out of but did not allow anyone to see inside.

The front yard was surrounded by an old iron fence about three feet tall. An old oak tree stood eerily in the middle of the small yard as though standing guard against the outside world. The grass yard was patchy and filled with high weeds. Energy surrounding the house was sad and gloomy. I could sense spirits in the house and knew there had been much agony brought upon the dark structure.

At the time of this visit it was somewhat difficult to get much history on such a house. The locals were not quick to admit to the city's darker past. I stood out front hoping to receive some impression of what might have happened. I sensed children suffering, a fire, and death. There was some feeling that this house had catered to very angry men who hurt children.

As I tried to focus more, I was interrupted...

"Let it go. There is no purpose to this." I knew the voice immediately but could not understand why Yeshua would try to deter me from finding out the secrets of this house. "Not everything is for you to know or to understand.

Things happen in life that set the tone for other events. Death has her mission as do you and I."

"So I am supposed to ignore some cries for help? I'm supposed to walk away when I sense a place like this?" I had always thought my gift was to simply learn about these places and record them for history to some degree.

"He is gone and will not answer." The cold gravelly voice sounded like the darkest growl of the cruelest demon. "I won't answer either."

"Pariah?" I was stunned. It was Pariah. He was standing in the shadows of the old tree. This was the first time he had actually talked to me in a way, communicating more than his name.

"Pariah? Hmmm, I guess that's as good a name as any." He seemed almost proud that I had called him that.

"Why are you here? Why do you follow me around?" I felt like I was in some type of trance.

"Why are YOU here? Maybe you are following me." He was acting smug. "You have much more to learn and much more to lose. I will give you this…you are heading in a direction you cannot change!"

"What is that supposed to mean?" I did not like this creature. I did not like his attitude. But for the first time ever, I was not afraid of him.

"Pariah? Hmmm…." And with that he vanished into the darkness of the tree.

I stood in a state of confusion. What was happening that I did not understand? How was it that I had three strong entities in my life and no one else seemed to ever even mention such things? I turned around and walked back to the square where Adrienne was, thinking the whole way about these events and how they impact my life.

I met back up with my friend around 6:00 p.m. I decided not to mention the afternoon's events to her. We enjoyed a nice dinner and listened to music for a bit on Bourbon Street. After sunset, we made our way down to the moonwalk that connected the Crescent City to the "Big Muddy."

Back then there was neither the casino nor the grand walkway that exist today. We found a spot on the boardwalk to sit where we could take in the breeze from the river. Nocturnal creatures began to journey out and the sounds of the city gave way to the soft sounds of night. It wasn't long before the night air blowing across the river began to softly mist.

"I'm jealous, you know." Adrienne was somewhat solemn this evening. "I wish I could do what you do. It must be such a rush to see ghosts and to talk to them."

"It's not exactly as fun as you might think. I mean I do wish that I could show people some of the things I see, but sometimes I have to deal with things you can't imagine." My thoughts reflected back to earlier in the day while Adrienne continued,

"It just seems like it would be so cool to see the things you see and help people communicate with loved ones who have passed away." Suddenly, Adrienne had my total attention! She said something that I had never thought of.

"Do you really think I could use this gift to connect people with the other side? I mean, seriously, I wouldn't have a clue on what to do to help people that way." But even as I spoke the words, I knew I was intrigued by the thought.

"Well, there are people called 'mediums' who claim they can do such a thing. They do séances, and walk through haunted houses, and communicate with the spirits. Jean Dixon claims to do this. There is a researcher and author named Hans Holzer who writes about her and others. How about Edgar Cayce? Supposedly, he communicates in a sleep trance." Adrienne had researched this, and I felt sure she was intent on helping me figure out my mission. She continued, "You need to go to the library and read about this stuff."

Adrienne had given me even more to think about. Was I a "Medium?" Could I use this gift to help people find closure? Should I even consider doing such a thing? Life had suddenly gotten a lot more complicated.

As the mist grew gently and began its slow march inland, we were engulfed by its mystic energy. We stood and slowly made our way towards the Basilica. The foggy mist surrounded our feet reaching up to our knees and gave our walk a mystical feel. As we reached Jackson Square, it felt as though we had gone back in time to the early 1700's when the city had first been built. We walked along the side streets amidst the old townhomes and began to sense the roaming spirits of the Quarter.

When we reached Decatur Street, we turned right and proceeded to Esplanade Avenue. As we came to Saint Philip Street, I noticed a dark figure across the street standing in front of a home on the corner. I recognized him immediately as the shadow man that I had seen earlier in the day. His glaring black eyes pierced the mist with an icy stare. Then he disappeared. I didn't say anything to Adrienne because the Pariah was definitely not part of New Orleans. I had long ago realized he was my own personal ghost.

"Oh, my God!" Adrienne broke the night's silence with a loud gasp. For a brief moment, I thought she had seen the shadow man. "What's that?"

She stood in awe and pointed down the street. A cluster of spirits who appeared to be Civil War soldiers were marching in the street towards us. We stood shock still as they came upon us and passed through us as though we did not exist. Seven battle worn soldiers, whispering among themselves, continued on with their endless march... past me... past Adrienne.

"I got to see them! You did it!" Adrienne hugged me tightly and jumped up and down in the street. "That is so cool! Oh my God! They were so real!"

I didn't have the heart to tell her that as far as I knew, I didn't do a thing. She seemed so happy in that moment to finally have experienced a bit of my world.

As quickly as the spirit soldiers had appeared, they were gone. Adrienne and I decided to turn left onto Barracks Street. We walked a block and began to hear music from a concertina squeeze box. In the mist we saw what had to be an old ship's captain singing in a language Adrienne believed to be Portuguese. He was a short and squat little man with a scarred face and limp. For a moment he looked directly at us and then seemed to simply fade into the fog.

"I don't know how you are doing this, but I am so happy! This is amazing!" Adrienne looked happier than I have ever seen her.

"I hate to admit it, but I'm not doing anything. I don't know how it is you can suddenly see these spirits." I was totally bewildered.

"Hmmm... maybe, at times, we all can see them? I guess your energy might make it easier for people around you to zone into them?" Adrienne was such an incredibly intelligent woman!

"I guess that's as good an explanation as any." It sounded like good reasoning to both of us.

We followed Barracks Street up to Dauphine Street and turned left back towards the old church on Orleans Street. The church had been the site of several events that were rumored to be less than Christian. It had also been a collection point for bodies that were found in local homes during one of the great fires. As we approached, the energy became heavy and sadness hung in the night air.

We walked up to the old church and were met by several spirits roaming about like zombies. They meandered aimlessly in search of some final resting place near a church where they could not find refuge. We watched as they repeated their nightly trek as though in some patterned dance macabre. The fog became thicker so we decided to head back to Adrienne's apartment.

I couldn't sleep that night and found myself out on the balcony sipping coffee and thinking about the last few days' events. The mist was in the streets like some alien cloud. The only sounds were the night's song and an occasional whistle of a river boat clearing the docks.

I was so wrapped in my thoughts that it took a few minutes before I realized I was being watched. Down the street and across the way, Pariah stood with his black glaring eyes. He stood there staring at me. For the first time I felt that he was trying to make some level of contact with me other than just trying to scare me.

He stood there with a look on his face I had never noticed before. In an odd way, it scared me more than when I was a child. It was as though he knew something he was not allowed to tell. He was like a harbinger of bad news and for the first time; he looked like the pariah that had been cast out into a world where he had no place to go. In a moment, he vanished into the mist. I went back to bed unable to rid myself of Pariah's stare and had a restless sleep.

I woke up early the next morning and spent most of it with Adrienne. We made love and sipped coffee as the sun rose gently into the morning sky. We took a walk along the Mississippi River and, in that moment, I realized I had found my Heartmate; that person who filled my heart and soul with deep and honest love. When I was with her I never felt an ounce of loneliness. My heart and soul was full. I knew marrying her would be my greatest adventure and truest love. We were ready to marry and she decided that while I was gone she would begin planning our wedding!

She dropped me off at the train station with a kiss and a promise to catch up with me in Alexandria on Tuesday when her vacation started. Even though we were going to Chicago to meet my parents in a few days, I felt like I wanted to stay there and hold her forever!

"I love you, Adrienne." I knew I needed to tell her what was in my heart. "You are my heart and soul. You bring me peace and a feeling of being a part of this world we live in. I will love you forever!"

Adrienne replied, "I have loved you from the first time we met. Mother told me after you left that we would meet again. She said that we all find the people we need in our lives when they matter the most if we just let things happen." We stood there holding each other and the world was right.

The announcement came to board my train. After one more Kiss and a warm embrace, I pulled myself away and boarded. I sat by the window, found where Adrienne was standing, and we waved goodbye to each other until the train left the station. My heart was full, and I already couldn't wait to be back in her arms.

CHAPTER TWENTY:

A Dream of Heaven

The train ride home was uneventful, so I got comfortable and caught a nap.

I fell asleep quickly and ended up having a really horrible nightmare. In the nightmare I was in a train collision. Events played out in slow motion around me. No voice to scream. Simply watching as death came for me. Watching as my life slipped away.... and then...A great white light.

I wandered for what seemed an eternity on occasion being greeted by a loved one long departed. Love and wisdom exchanged hands as we moved on our separate ways.

I came to what suddenly appeared as a clearing in the woods on the side of a mountain. The air was crisp and cool with a waterfall gently introducing itself to a glistening lake. There were beautiful flowers from white roses to bright pansies. Animals big and small were meandering about as though there was some mystic level of coexistence.

On the lake was a small but serene log cabin. In its simplicity was its beauty. Smoke dancing from the chimney and a vegetable garden outside the door. I knew I was home. I could feel it. The geese were flying overhead in a honking chorus and cardinals were calling to each other in harmony.

I walked to the water and saw koi swimming in a rainbow dance of elegant precision. I felt the water, and it was both refreshing and warm to the touch. Across the way I saw elk, moose and deer grazing alongside the bear, wolf and hawks.

A gentle woman came to greet me. It was Azrael, the Angel of Death. She held in her hand a small flower... a forget-me-not... Appropriate, I thought. As we walked a ways together, she seemed to sing a song whose lyrics I cannot remember and yet shall never forget. We walked to the cabin; and as she went upon her journey, I remembered that she was not to be feared nor disrespected.

I entered the cabin and was met by a myriad of emotion, my senses exploding in a pageant of remembrance, taking in those aromas and smells that always remind me of a lost loved one or a fond moment. I was enveloped in rose, lemon, Camilla and patchouli, accompanied by those special soft sounds that always comfort and strength.

From the woods came a familiar bark as Silky emerged, still a pup filled with curiosity and wonder. Grampa came behind her with a fishing pole in hand and Great Grandma by his side. I knew I was home. I knew now where Eden was. I saw behind them a woman in a white veil. She seemed familiar, but I couldn't see her clearly. She smiled through the laced curtain and let me know that I would not be alone in my eternal heart as well.

I woke up abruptly. The dream made me uneasy, and I couldn't wait to get off the bus to share it with Adrienne. The bus pulled into the station. After I got my bags, I located a phone and called Adrienne to let her know that I had arrived home and to tell her about my dream; but, she didn't answer.

I waited a bit, and then finally got her answering machine. As I left a message, her sister picked up the phone. Adrienne had gotten into a car accident on her way home and died at the scene. My nightmare had been a premonition. I would never again have even a moment with this special woman whom I had grown to love.

My heart ached and tears rolled down my face as I turned from the phone and found a place to sit. My spirit faded and I felt nothing but cold harsh loneliness. My feelings of love slipped away into the darkness of dispair and soulful pain. She was gone. I was alone. This was my Heartmate. How could such a thing happen? I knew heartmates were eternal connections that would be connected to us forever. It hurt so deeply that I cried. I didn't care who saw me and I didn't ask for help. I cried until I had no tears left. I don't remember how long I was there nor when I stood up to leave.

As I walked towards the hotel from the payphone, I also realized to my horror that the shadow creature had known.

That was what I saw in his eyes. I was horrified, and I was angry beyond comprehension! I didn't want this evil spirit to ever show itself again. Whatever it was; it had no place in my life. I was determined to find a way to block it!

CHAPTER TWENTY-ONE:

Adrienne's Spirit

Adrienne's family asked me to join in the funeral procession and to say a few words. I had never experienced a New Orleans Jazz Funeral but knew immediately it was exactly what Adrienne would have wanted.

A small ensemble jazz band would lead the procession with a heartfelt blues song. Six local artists and friends had volunteered to carry the casket through the streets from the old church to the cemetery. On one block all would march in sync to the music carefully lined up front and back, and then on the next block the musicians would break into wild jazz music. Everyone would break stride and dance to whatever beat they felt. The dancing would continue until the music changed and the solemnness of the occasion was acknowledged.

At the cemetery several folks talked followed by singing. Finally, it was my turn to speak. My heart was heavy, and my legs were weak. I spoke from my heart and let the spirit speak through me.

"Years ago when I performed my first funeral, I tried very hard to find the right words to say. That one thing that would take away the pain; I never found it. Not in all of these years have I ever been able to tell someone the words that would make losing someone they care about easier. The fact is death is not easy." I took a moment to catch my breath.

"A person is so many things to so many people; each person embracing a memory or a moment in time that holds the lost loved one in their heart forever- a trip across country, a special date, or a dance across the Chicago River on a cool March Morning. We see each other so differently and as such easing a mourning heart is never so easy as a single word or phrase.

"I have learned through the years to suggest that people mourn their loved one for a moment in time and then celebrate that person's life forever. Mourn the loss of that person's smile but never forget it. Mourn the passing of days when that dear soul is not near but celebrate the times they were. Mourn the days when we cannot make new memories but embrace those that were indeed created." I felt these words come from deep within.

"Life should be measured by how well we traveled through it, what lessons we learn and which lessons we teach. Life is the greatest journey we can have, and it is up to each of us to set the course. We can change our destiny but not our fate. That is God's way. There is no rhyme or reason to when and where we pass. It is simply our fate." A few members of the procession called out Amen and Praise to the Lord.

"Fate: That final moment when we reach our life destination. That moment when we realize we have completed this journey and are now free to become one spirit with God."

The old black hymns combined with the Creole songs and merged with kind words from friends and soulful preaching. As I stood there, I knew in my heart that Adrienne would have loved it.

"Of course, I love it! It's not about death but about moving forward. It's about escaping the shackles of this world to fly free in the next."

"Adrienne?" Had my grief finally caused me to lose it?

"No, Babe, you're ok. It's me. I can only stay a moment, but I will be back."

"I love you so much. I am sorry I didn't save you. I just didn't realize it in time." My guilt came forward like lightening. I had to let her know how I felt.

"I love you, too! You need to understand that you could not change this. This is my fate; my time." Her energy shone through me right into my heart. "We are all given a certain amount of time here. It is ever so important that we use it as well as possible."

"Adrienne, I was given a sign that you would die, and I didn't realize it...."

"What makes you think you could have changed what happened? That's your grief and ego talking. I hate to tell you this, but you have the ability to see when people will die. It does not mean you can change it or even that you should." Even in death Adrienne was teaching me things.

"I think you will find that the hardest part of your gift is to witness some events that you have no say in. If you try too hard to change things, people will see you are different. Do you want to be an outcast?" It seemed as though she was warning me more than anything.

"There are things in this universe for you to learn. I will help when I can. I have to go now. I must cross over to begin my new journey and learn how to exist in this new life. I won't be gone long." With that she gave me a kiss and vanished into the veil.

I stood there a moment relishing that kiss and still feeling it gently upon my lips. A tear fell softly down my cheek coming to a rest just at the edge of my face. I closed my eyes in silent prayer and thankfulness that I had been able to talk to Adrienne. I stood motionless in time for a moment until a misty rain began to fall and the soft raindrops awakened me.

I was lost. My heartmate was taken from me and I was alone. I fulfilled my obligation to the little church and walked away from that level of my ministry. I was not a Preacher. I was becoming a historian of sorts. I had begun to gather spirits and help people find some closure to the loss of their loved ones.

I had four months to finish out the lease on our apartment. Then I decided to return to Chicago. At this point my plans weren't clear, but I knew that I had an interesting life ahead.

CHAPTER TWENTY-TWO:

The Houma Plantation

After the death of my Heartmate, Adrienne; I stayed in Louisiana for a few months and I found myself just floating from haunting to haunting. I am not sure why. I think I was hoping that she would show herself to me. That we could talk again and I would know I had not truly ever lost her. She promised she would be back and she always kept her promises.

Before I left Louisiana for Illinois, I joined a group of friends on a trip to Houma. We were going on a swamp tour and staying at an old plantation home that belonged to a friend's parents. This home had been in the family for three generations and sat majestically at the edge of the swamp. We had been invited for the weekend to enjoy a "mudbug boil" and Cajun/Creole style gathering.

Houma was typical of southern towns of the 1980's in that it was not overly developed and very conservative. We arrived in town early so we stopped to grab a quick bite and soft drink at a small café. As we were strangers in town we were met with polite stares and what felt like a level of suspicion. It did not help that one of the couples in our group was interracial.

The café was a nice little place. Like most eateries of the time, it was filled with old men and the local loafers. Two young girls were sipping bottled Pepsi and munching peanuts across from two boys enjoying hamburgers and shakes. Our waitress, Millie, was a middle aged woman that seemed life tired but determined to make it through her day.

"What brings you kids to Houma?" she asked.

"We are going on a swamp tour and staying at an old plantation," Linda chimed in. Linda was a friendly person by nature.

"Well, that will be fun for you. I grew up by the swamps, and they are kind of neat... dangerous too. Watch out for gators." Millie seemed nice enough. "Now, what are you kids going to eat?"

We all ordered burgers and cokes before starting conversations about our various lives. Instead of joining in, I sat and listened to the typical chatter. Soon we had finished our meal.

After eating, we walked about town to stretch our legs before heading to the manor where we would stay. I noticed what looked like an odd shrine in the window of the hardware store. We walked over to get a closer look, and there in the window was a display dedicated to what was called the Rougarou.

The Rougarou appeared to be a swamp creature- part man, part wolf, and somewhat swampy. There were several poorly drawn pictures and artist renditions that seemed to offer a cross composite of what the creature might look like.

"Looks like Lon Chaney, Jr. in the Wolf man movies." I always had a habit of associating things with old movies.

"This one looks more like Big Foot!" said Dave, who was fairly short in stature but carried himself pretty big.

"Looks like a bad attempt to get people to visit and spend money," replied Barry, who was cynical about everything.

"Well, you never know what is out there in the universe. Let's get going." I had learned to never close my mind to anything.

The ride to the plantation home was uneventful and brief. As we approached the manor, I noticed it was a magnificent two story antebellum mansion typical of the region. There were old trees covered with moss and a long dirt drive ending in a turnaround in front of the building. The manor had 12 bedrooms, several large gathering rooms, and a huge kitchen. The grounds were dotted with barns, sheds, and the remains of old sharecropper homes.

I had been told that these homes had been converted from old slave shanties.

We were all assigned rooms and then took some time to relax before meeting in the main parlor. Our hosts were Cajuns, and it took a bit for us to fully get the dialect so we could follow all they were saying. As they discussed the swamp tour with us, I began to notice an older woman who was standing at a doorway leading to another room off the parlor.

Immediately, I knew that she was more than likely a spirit attached to the house. This older woman seemed curious about why we were there; I watched her slowly begin walking amongst everyone. As she approached me, we locked eyes, and I knew she realized I could sense her presence. Quickly, the spirit vanished for a moment; then came back and stared at me for a bit. I knew she wasn't the only spirit in the house or on the grounds because I had felt everything from Plantation owners, to slaves, to Indians when we drove in.

The family seemed very nice and happy to be able to share their home with us. It wasn't until we all sat down to dinner that they informed us of the many ghosts that had been seen on the grounds and in the house, unaware that this was not entirely new information for me.

I decided to test my skills a bit and deliberately opened up to any energy that might choose to visit. I have to admit I

147

was curious to see what might happen and who might show.

I immediately asked the older woman who she was.

"My name is Elizabeth, and I am the great grandmother of the man who owns this place."

"How long have you been here?" I asked.

"I moved here when I was a little girl and lived here until my death at 95 years old."

I sensed that she was perhaps the most active spirit around us and had been seen many times by family and guests. "Are you trapped here? Can you leave?" I was curious why she would choose to stay in this place instead of going forward.

"I am here by choice. We all are. No one is ever trapped here. We either go through the veil and return or we stay for one reason or another." She seemed almost blasé about it. "I have to go."

I wished her well and rejoined the conversation. The owners had listed a variety of ghosts and even let us know where they could be found. We were given freedom to explore the house and grounds while waiting for the picnic they were preparing. Immediately, my friends Linda and Dave joined me, and we made our way outside to the old buildings.

The largest building we came to was a storage barn for cotton, complete with a baler and baled cotton. As you might guess, the stacks of cotton bales managed to sound proof inner areas of the building. We walked around in the unnatural quiet until we heard a sound coming from behind a stack of cotton bales.

"Do you hear that?" Linda became aware of it first.

"It sounds like a baby!" Dave walked to the bales and began searching.

We searched the entire building and found nothing. As we made a second sweep of the place, we began to hear what sounded like an old hymn right out of the spiritual South. We looked and looked but could not find where it was coming from. Finally, we just moved on to the next building.

When we reached the shanty huts, a sense of sadness overwhelmed us, and my companions chose not to enter the houses. I walked through the door of the smaller hut by myself, feeling the humid steam brought about by the heat of the midday sun striking down. The air itself seemed heavy. I caught my breath and proceeded to investigate this two room shack. The presence of spirits filled each room, but one soul stood out the most.

I sensed a tall stocky male whose energy suggested he was the guardian of these souls, probably either the father or

149

alpha male of a family of slaves or sharecroppers. He stood in the dark watching me as I looked around. All through the house I noticed the smell of charred wood and smoke. Later, I found out an entire family had died when a wood stove caught fire. The shanty I was in had been rebuilt out of the salvaged wood and old buildings from a local farm.

I walked through a few other buildings until I came to what felt like a gathering place. It might have been used as a store to allow the sharecroppers to shop and use credit against their week's work. It may have been used as a church as well. The feeling of frustration mixed with prayer permeated the place. I could hear old hymns whispering in the wind around the house. At the back of this space, I could see an old man who had the energy of a minister around him. He looked at me a moment, smiled, and wandered away.

The last spot Linda, Dave, and I were drawn to was an overgrown field surrounded by a broken down fence long in need of repair. At first I wasn't sure what we were looking at, but it felt like a graveyard. Later, I learned that it was a "Blacks Only" cemetery. A few old stone markers were strewn about, but for the most part the graves were unmarked. I sensed spirits of all ages buried there. I also sensed there had been beatings, hangings, and other unnecessary deaths!

All in all, the spirits I found and the energy I experienced were typical of old plantations with varied histories. Unfortunately, I hadn't discovered anything unusual. It was time to head back to the plantation house and settle in for the night.

As the sun set and the moon began to rise, we heard the choir of nocturnal animals all around us. As we saw the lights of the house, we began to have the feeling we were being followed. Then, as we reached the steps up to the grand porch, we heard the hideous howl of some wild creature rising from the swamp.

CHAPTER TWENTY-THREE:

The Rougarou

When I was a kid I loved a comic book about a man who had been turned into a swamp creature called Swamp Thing. It was a cool relief from the usual superhero books of the day. This story took place in the town of Houma, Louisiana and the creature was involved in a variety of natural and supernatural events.

It wasn't until my visit to the old plantation that I found out that in a sense the Swamp Thing was indeed "real." It occurred to me that Swamp Thing was derived from the legends of the Rougarou like we had seen at the hardware store in town. I didn't imagine in my wildest thoughts that I would ever encounter such a creature.

The wild hideous growl we heard coming from the mossy covered oak grove sent shivers through us all. This howl was a cross between a wolf and some tormented humanlike creature. As we reached the safety of the porch, we noticed the air smelled like putrid rotting meat and felt like evil's hot breath. We turned to gaze into the deep darkness of the woods only to see two piercing red eyes glaring back at us.

"What is that?"

"The eyes are glowing red!"

"What's that smell?"

"It sounds like it's hurt!"

"Somebody get a gun!"

"It's horrible!"

We all reacted at once as our host and the property caretaker came out of the house sporting shotguns. They said it was nothing to worry about, and we should all go inside.

Someone suggested that a swamp dog had gotten away from its owner and was out prowling for a midnight meal. I was raised a hunter and knew the difference between a hungry dog and a creature out to render something apart for the sheer carnage of it.

We went inside and sat in the parlor for a while before hearing a knock at the door. Several well-armed men were there; the owner then walked off into the woods with them. I knew this was more than they were saying, so I walked into the kitchen to get a cup of coffee and interrupted the staff talking about the evening's happenings. It was their general belief that the plantation was being stalked by a Rougarou.

The cook said, "The Rougarou was a poor soul who resorted to cannibalism and was doomed to hunt for 101 days; then any person it had drawn blood from would have the curse transferred to them."

"It's like a werewolf!" The maid exclaimed, seeming pretty sure of her description.

The cook's assistant was Creole and remembered hearing something from her grandfather. "It's like a Wendigo from French Canadian folklore. A poor soul trapped in a hideous body unable to free itself." Quietly, I took my coffee and walked back to the parlor.

The hunting party returned around midnight to meet with a local fellow who had brought his bloodhounds. Obviously, they were going out again, so I asked to go along. After answering a few questions about gun safety and hunting, I was welcomed to join the group. The owner gave me spare swamp boots and clothing more appropriate to wear in the swamps. We left around 1 a.m. and headed towards the deeper part of the swamp.

The tracking dogs seemed to be drawn to the bayou area. As we neared the swamp, we began to hear that howling noise again. Something large was crashing through the brush ahead of us. We did find tracks, but they didn't make any sense to me. They seemed too big for a canine animal and were oddly human-like. We were moving quickly with the dogs and then came to a sudden halt.

"What's going on?" One of the men asked.

"The dogs are acting odd, like they sense something," another voice said.

That's when we heard the monstrous growl coming from a few yards away in the dark swamp willows. The dogs went quiet at first; then began to whine and tug at the leashes in the owner's hand. They were afraid and wanted to run. I understood the impact of this immediately! These dogs that had been trained to track wolf and bear were afraid.

In the distance there was a silhouette in the edge of the shadows. Some said it was like a high heap of swamp weed shaped like a man; others said it looked like a giant wolf standing on its hind legs.

To me it looked more like a man whose body had been contorted and bent as though some birth defect had twisted him. He was hidden mostly in the shadows, but his eyes struck out from the dark like red hot coals. His teeth were broken and jagged in a way that made him look vicious. He stood another moment as though he was gathering our scents, and then he vanished into the swamp. No one moved.

It was a minute or two before the sounds of the swamp returned, and we all began breathing normally again. You could feel the slight fear that permeated the night. We stood still while the sound of a creature running away from where we were, slowly, drifted into the darkness.

We had seen something in that swamp. Was it a hoax? Was it a Rougarou? We would never really know.

CHAPTER TWENTY-FOUR:

My Evolution

I returned to Illinois in hopes of finding a new focus. The ministry was not my path, and I was at a crossroads. I needed time to just catch my breath, so I got a job and tried to settle into a routine until I could create my life.

I was in Illinois about 3 months when I ran into my old girlfriend, Jen, at a gathering. We talked a bit and reminisced about the old days. She and I had visited a few of the more haunted sections of Chicago when we were younger. I left for Louisiana and she dated a fellow for a while, but he was into drugs, and it didn't work out. I told her about Adrienne and New Orleans.

"You're still doing that? I would think by now it would be getting pretty old. I mean, doesn't it get overwhelming for you?" She asked.

"Sometimes; mostly it is just natural to me to do it." I was fairly candid and explained to her how things had evolved in the last few years. "It's not like it was when we were kids. My sensing works differently now. I understand it more and know how to have some control over it."

"What about the shadow creature that followed you around? Is he still there?" She seemed concerned for me.

"He still is. I'm beginning to figure him out more but still don't like him being around." I was happy to have someone to talk to. "I don't think he is good or bad, but I do know he seems to foreshadow bad things."

"Well, isn't that kind of good? I mean at least you get a warning." Jen was trying to look at the positive side of this.

"That's the problem. I don't know something bad will occur until it's about to happen, and then I can't do anything to prevent it. He is like some harbinger of bad news." I felt sad just thinking about it. "If I say anything to anyone, then I become an outcast."

"You can't live this way. Walk away from it." Jen was almost crying. "Why is it your job? Turn it off and live a normal life."

Jen made a lot of sense to me that day. How nice it would be to just turn it off, walk away, and never deal with it again. After all, I was not the only one who had the gift. I was not the only one who could use it. Maybe it was time to step aside and be normal.

I went home that night with a lot on my mind. Would it be possible that I could just shut it off and move on? Did I even know what normal was anymore?

I woke up the next morning with my mind made up. I had decided it was time to walk away from it all. I went to the Army Recruiting office and signed up. No more ghosts or walk-throughs and definitely no more communicating with the dead.

Jen had been my first love and those old feelings came back with a fury. Whether it was true love or a need to be loved; Jen and I got married a few months later and life began again. I had evolved past those days of ghost hunting and spirits. Now my days were filled with simple pleasures and a happy wife. I was experiencing the life I used to think I would have and wanted it to go on and on. And I almost made it… until the time came for me to leave for basic training.

"Don't go! You are allowed to change your mind. If you go, nothing will be the same." Jen was crying as we waited for the recruiter to pick me up to take me to the train.

"I am obligated. I have to go. It's only a few months, and then I'll be home." I tried my best to comfort her.

"I just have a feeling that if you go, I will lose you." I could feel the fear in her words.

"It'll be ok. I will be back in a few months, and we will go on a nice vacation." I didn't know what else to say. The truth was I had the same feeling.

We lay in bed for a while longer; then got up and had breakfast. We didn't say much but hugged over and over. Time seem to drag slowly as we waited for my ride. When the car finally pulled up, Jen began to cry again. I held her tight for as long as I could; then I watched her. As we pulled away, my heart felt a little empty. It was as though the universe had pulled me away from my happiness.

CHAPTER TWENTY-FIVE:

The Gangs All Here

I left for basic training in January, and as I headed to Fort Dix in New Jersey, I was not happy. I should not be there. I was supposed to be a minister and have a nice little church somewhere. Jen and I were supposed to have children and be happy. This was not a part of our plans, and Jen had made it very clear that she hated my decision to enlist.

It wasn't a horrible winter, and the weather was tolerable. I was hoping basic training would offer me the opportunity to rid my mind of anything except learning to be a soldier. I did my best to let go of my independence and free my mind, but I was feeling angry and disillusioned. The world was making me cynical. Between the people I had to deal with and the fact that I had to leave my wife behind, I was struggling. Add to that the fact that I had not planned on the lack of sleep and overabundance of physical therapy. I was losing my faith and my spirituality.

By the end of the second week of training, exposure to rain and varying cold temperatures put me in the hospital with pneumonia. I was near death and defenseless to spiritual attacks. As I lay in bed, I thought at first I was hallucinating, but soon realized that something more was happening.

Pariah stood in the corner at the far end of the room. Yeshua was standing by me, and Azrael was literally at the door.

"What's going on?" I wondered. I looked at Yeshua hoping he would offer me some comfort.

"You are ok. She isn't here for you," he said, smiling at me.

"So why are you all here?" I needed to know.

"You can't blame yourself for things you cannot change, and you can't blame anyone for what happens along your path," Death spoke sincerely but pointedly. "You cannot avoid your true path for long either."

"Your path was written long ago just as our paths were," Pariah explained, seeming to take pleasure in telling me I had no choice.

"We all have left the road before us more than once, but we must fulfill our missions. It's not about us. It's about synchronicity." Yeshua spoke simply but made his point.

162

"We are too many souls to walk away. You can't walk away."

"We will be with you all your life. There is nothing you can do to change this...even in death." Pariah came closer.

"Pariah!!!" Both Azrael and Yeshua called out as a warning.

"He needs to know and the sooner the better!" Pariah growled at them and then vanished.

"Don't mind him. That is why he is an outcast. He cannot leave well enough alone. Just let what is meant to be; happen. Your life is a continuous lesson, and each moment becomes a chapter in the universe." Yeshua smiled again and vanished.

Then Azrael smiled at me, "We need to talk. Go to sleep. We will chat."

She slowly disappeared into the shadows. I stared at the ceiling for a time and then drifted off to sleep, feeling angry and somewhat disappointed with life.

CHAPTER TWENTY-SIX:

Walking with Death

I awoke later that night in a field of beautiful flowers, the variety changing with every breeze. It was the most incredible sight. I stood in the Elysian Field...Homer's meadow, where the favored of the Gods live in perfection. The subtle sweet smell of these flowers lifted my spirit. Suddenly, I felt a presence. I knew it was her before she even began to speak.

"You needed to visit. Lately, you have become cynical and outright judgmental. That cannot be your way."

I turned to see her as though for the first time, a vision of perfect imperfection as I knew was right, her reddish brunette hair blowing wistfully in the slight spring breeze, and her skin milky white and glowing. Seeing her made me feel as though my life might have meaning, and I was being rewarded by her presence, my life Angel! She may have been a fool's vision, but one I needed at that moment.

"You are angry. You are losing Faith. You don't catch your breath anymore. You just seem to be moving about blindly. You created a place where you would be happy, your version of Heaven. You don't visit your Heaven much anymore. Why is that?" She touched my shoulder and glanced at me with the warmth of a mother.

"Sorry, I just haven't felt that it was the place for me these days. People are changing. They've lost their moral compass." I sighed, knowing I say little when I am with her. I simply and concisely say what I have to say.

"But you already know that the world has to be lost before Heaven can be found, so why would you want to fight that change?" Her questions always seemed more like statements to me.

"I guess I did not know the toll it would take on me. I guess I just didn't realize how it would affect me. Everywhere I go, I feel people's desperation, loss of Faith; and, in many cases, I feel their souls giving up. We worship the wrong things." I knew I was just rambling, but I felt I had to get it all off my chest.

"We show sadness at the loss of strangers, and yet many show so much less compassion for members of their own family. In one breath, they condemn a family member and in the next praise some stranger they barely know; if they even know him at all. We are out of sync with what is truly important. Our sense of morality is so askew."

Death stood there listening as I continued.

"One man admits a crime and receives a slap on the wrist. When he dies, they have a grand memorial. Another man is told of a crime, reports it to the proper authority, and

165

because he does not check to see if it was taken care of, he is demonized. His career is tarnished. When he dies, it's a silent and solemn affair. Tell me, in what world is this right?"

Death looked puzzled for a moment. "You really are hurting. It's never been your job to save the world. He is here for that. Besides, considering the outcome of that job, do you really want it?"

"I just am tired of watching the bad guys win and society praise them for it. If you are famous enough or rich enough, you can perform any act or indignity and get away with it. People have begun to overlook transgressions against the world just because the people performing them accomplished one or two grand feats. Somehow, this seems to mean we should overlook their crimes." I was determined to make my point.

"I am not saying we should not forgive people, but I am saying they should not be elevated to some great stature either. Society has begun to accept dope heads, pedophiles, and profiteering politicians as though their behaviors are the norm. We now have separate standards for common people and the well-to-do. I am sickened every time one of these 'special' individuals dies or is caught in yet another transgression and the public simply lets it slide because they are rich or famous. When I see people praising these criminals, I get angry. I just lose a little more Faith."

Azrael gave me that look that always lifted my spirits. "Has it ever occurred to you that this is all a test? That each person's approach to each of these events will determine the path they follow? Consider that how easily someone surrenders their morality determines how tough and how miserable their life may be?"

As we began walking towards a wooded area, Death continued to speak.

"You already know life is a test, more for the individual than anything. This isn't about standing before God in judgment. It's about living on earth in happiness and self-contentment. You have to let this go and worry about yourself. Every person must first create their own path and find their own way before they can look around to see what is true in this world."

"So I am supposed to be selfish?" Guess I didn't quite understand.

"Not at all, but you cannot and are not responsible for what other people choose to think or to do. If they want to worship some famous person despite the evil that person may have done, then they have that right, and you have NO right to tell them otherwise. Live your life, and let others live theirs...you have said this a hundred times. Let it go. You have things to do, and this is not productive to what you are here for." Death became stern when she made this last comment.

"You know this spot is my Heaven, and it's almost perfect for me, except there is no water" Even before I had finish speaking, I heard the soft splashing of water on the shore and smelled the wood burning in the fireplace of my cabin.

"Nice change of subject...Your Heaven is always here for you. You created it. It's still mostly the same. Perhaps the woods have gotten a little darker and the water somewhat deeper, but it is the heaven you are creating. Go. Think about what I have said. You will awaken soon. Sometimes it's important to get away from the world and think."

As I walked towards the cabin, she yelled out one more bit of wisdom. "You won't save the world, and there is no sense trying. You have people to save, and people who will save you...just like everyone else. Never raise yourself above another person nor lower yourself to them. Be at Peace."

I don't remember leaving my little piece of Heaven, but it wasn't long before I woke up. I lay there with my thoughts and knew that I would never be able to have a normal life. My gift was my birthright, and like it or not; I had to follow that path.

When I called Jen, she was not happy and told me that I shouldn't make a decision until I was out of the military. I told her I would make the Army my priority. I think we both knew that that was not a promise I could keep. We didn't realize that my gift was a part of me that would not go away.

CHAPTER TWENTY-SEVEN:

Philadelphia and a Founding Father

In the middle of basic training we were allowed to take a four day weekend pass. My squad and I decided to take a trip to Philadelphia to see the historic sites there. We stayed at an older hotel in town and were lucky enough to have a squad member with us who had relatives in the area.

I took a break before we left on our tour and called Jen. We talked for a while; then I said goodnight. I could feel coldness from her. She said she didn't want to be married to someone people would laugh at. I was not sure what I was going to do. All I knew was that I had to decide my path soon.

"You know you are going to lose her, don't you?" Pariah said, standing nearby in the shadow of the old staircase. "She doesn't want to be with a weirdo... an outcast. This is just the beginning."

"Why the hell do you take such pleasure in my misery?" I wanted to beat him senseless.

"Trust me. It's no pleasure, just the truth. You already decided to follow this path when you let us into your life. You have no clue what is ahead of you." He was staring into me and beyond. "Remember...you chose this."

Before I could say another word, he was gone. I felt like my life as I had hoped it would be had already died. There was only emptiness.

I walked back to the room where everyone was meeting for the tour. My heart wasn't into sightseeing, but I also didn't want to be alone, so I went with the group as planned. It had been decided that we would see the Liberty Bell and other revolutionary sites, so our guide charted a great route and we set out to explore the city.

Our first stop was Independence Hall where the government began. This building was full of spirits. I found it interesting that I sensed a lot of energy there from slaves.

"All men are created equal; some, however seem more equal than others," I turned around and before me stood Ben Franklin. "My Masonic brothers would be amazed by you. I saw you before you even came into the building."

I knew that I gave off a glow on the other side and that very often it would attract spirits to me. He walked up to me and around me as though he was trying to decide if I was friend or foe.

"I like it here. Most of the others returned to their homes or such. For me, this place was life." He removed his glasses and continued to speak." Do you know they throw pennies at my grave? All because some fool misquoted me and now a "penny saved is a penny earned" is permission for people to disrespect my final resting place! When I am there, I throw the damned things back at them!"

"I didn't know that, but I will be careful not to ever do such a thing to anyone's grave." I honestly didn't know what else to say.

"Well then, be gone with you. I have things to do." And with that he vanished.

I looked to see if anyone else had seen the apparition, but noticed they were all busy looking at the various rooms. I saw the wisp of one or two other spirits, but for the most part, it was quiet.

We walked across the way to where the Liberty Bell was kept. What an incredible feeling to be in this place which was so instrumental in the formation of our government! All of us were quiet while standing by the bell, sharing the sacred moment.

Then we headed towards Washington Square. I knew nothing about this place, so finding out it had been a cemetery was a shock.

The history of the square is odd. It started out as a Potter's Field for the burial of poor people and strangers. At one point, it was found to be good grazing land and was used as a pasture. Then soldiers from the Revolutionary War were buried there. After that it was used by the British as a prison area for a while.

In the 1800's the land was converted to a park and eventually named after George Washington. There is a belief that many unmarked graves still remain. Some people have claimed to see a ghost named Leah roaming around watching over the graves to make sure no grave robbers disturb them.

As we entered the park, I began to sense and then see many spirits roaming about. There were slaves, soldiers, and people who were not welcomed by the church. There was a man named Carpenter who claimed to have owned the property at one time. The spirits just ambled about, and yet they had no desire to move on. No matter what I said, they chose to stay. I had encountered this before and knew to leave well enough alone. Since our guide wanted to take us to one last site, it seemed like a good time to be on our way.

We ended up at a place called Christ Church Burial Grounds. This is the resting place of a few signers of the Declaration of Independence, including... Ben Franklin! I have to admit that I was curious to see what was going to happen.

We entered the grounds. After a short walk around Franklin's grave, the guide immediately suggested tossing pennies! I glanced around to see if we had company, and sure enough…there stood Ben Franklin.

I don't remember who threw the first penny, but every penny tossed came flying back. How amazing! I stood back and watched the show. Mr. Franklin gave me a rather stern look before tossing a coin at me, but his aim was not very good, and I simply continued to laugh. It seemed to me that he actually enjoyed the interaction with this side as much as the penny flippers enjoyed it.

Since it was a nice night we all wanted a beer, so we decided to walk back to a pub near our hotel. After we got there, we sat sipping beer and talking about our day. I listened for a bit but eventually excused myself from the conversation and sat at the bar.

"Is it going to be like this all my life?' I thought to myself. "No matter where I go will they find me?"

I didn't sleep well that night. I just lay in bed staring out the window … wondering… thinking… Finally, I hit the point when I began to mourn. I realized that my path had already been decided, and I could not change it.

CHAPTER TWENTY-EIGHT:

Time

The next few years were a blur. I went through various training experiences in different places and had some minor encounters with the spirits. Jen and I got divorced. I completed my training and eventually ended up in Louisiana at Fort Polk. Overall, it seemed as though the universe had decided to leave me alone.

I settled in to life at Fort Polk, almost forgetting that I had a gift. I avoided New Orleans and the Quarter and anywhere else I might make contact with the spirits. Life was good. Adrienne was still deep within my heart but I had come to terms with losing her. I suppose I felt like I had actually found that normalcy I was looking for.

The first chance I got, I bought some fishing equipment and a license. Then I found a place called Toledo Bend Reservoir. The fishing was great, and the place was so big I could hide away from the world. I would bring a cooler filled with enough pop and sandwiches to last for the whole day. I thought I had figured it all out. If I couldn't lose my gift, I would avoid using it at all cost. This plan almost worked.

In order to create the reservoir, builders had to flood over 185,000 acres of land, including Time, Texas, which was a small town consisting of barely fifty people. This town contained a quaint church and a cemetery like most little towns. When the reservoir was decided upon, Time was declared condemned, and folks were either bought out or forced out.

One day while out on a small bass boat I floated over Time, though I didn't realize it at first. I was enjoying a beautiful sunny day in April, warm but not humid. As I sat in the boat eating crackers and bologna, I heard a voice.

"Go away!" It was the voice of an old man who acted as though I had spilled his checker board.

I ignored it. I steered my boat a little ways away and started fishing again.

"Go away!"

"I am not listening. I'm going to ignore the voice." I had forgotten that for them our thoughts are our voices.

"Go away! Go away! GO AWAY!!!"

Suddenly, the water became choppy and a cool wind began to blow. Clouds covered the sky, even though in the distance it was a beautiful day. The sound of several people mumbling surrounded me until I finally gave in. I turned the motor over and headed towards the better weather. Once I was far enough away, the area cleared up and the water calmed.

I told the attendant at the marina what had happened. He just shrugged his shoulders and replied, "You must have been near Time. Folks tend to stay away from there. Some folks say it's haunted."

I didn't say another word. I loaded my things into my Opal GT and sat for a moment before heading back to Fort Polk. It was annoying that I couldn't even enjoy quiet time without eventually running into *them*.

"You still don't get it, do you?" I knew in an instant that Adrienne was with me. "Has it occurred to you that you can tune them out? They need your permission to interact."

"I was only thinking about fishing!" I couldn't figure out what had happened.

"Really; 185,000 acres... and you just happened to stop right on top of a submerged town? What are the chances of that?" I had forgotten her polite sarcasm. In fact, I missed it very much. "You miss it. Admit it. Normal isn't for you. It never will be."

"You are right. And, Adrienne...I'm sorry I haven't stopped to visit you. I miss you." I could see her caramel skin and deep blue eyes with that wonderful sparkle in them.

"I've been here all along. You have to decide what you want. You will eventually be able to control this gift, but until then you either see us or you don't. Right now you can't have it both ways." Her voice had that tone to it... letting me know she was bound and determined to teach me whether I wanted to learn or not.

"So, for now, it's all or nothing?" I sighed. I had to admit that I really did want to follow this path but was resisting it because I didn't want to be attacked for my gift. I think the part of me that wanted to be a minister had something to do with my resistance.

"You need to let go of what you have been taught by society and trust your own spirituality. Remember Marie Laveau? She was Catholic but knew that she could help more people through the practice of voodoo. After all, many of the slaves back in her time did not fully understand Christianity nor were they welcome in the churches." Adrienne was becoming my guide from the spiritual realm.

"So, I can follow both paths to some extent but ultimately I have to have some foundation of faith." It's funny, but I think I knew that already.

"You don't have to choose. Your true nature and faith will come through. I mean either way this is where you are headed so isn't it better that YOU control when and how you do it?" She smiled at me and then gave me a hug. I could smell her jasmine perfume and feel the warmth from her soul. "Good bye, Dearest. I will be around."

I stood for a moment embracing her energy and then I said goodbye. "I love you."

I knew right then and there that I was going to follow my path and use my gifts. The problem was that I didn't really know how to go about it. I decided to go to the library and see what I could find on ghosts, mediums, and the supernatural. I decided if I was going to use my gift, then I would be the best there was!

CHAPTER TWENTY-NINE:

Just Perfect

The libraries had very little to offer and the book stores had sensationalized crap. Television had "In search of..." or similar tripe. How could I do this if I didn't know what to do?

"Stop! You will drive yourself crazy!" Yeshua said, appeared next to me in the old library. "You are not going to be perfect. You are going to miss things or assume things. That's natural."

"I am just afraid I will hurt someone or mislead someone." I felt a little lost.

"People make choices. If they choose to see you or anyone else it is their choice. No one is perfect...not even me!" His honesty had a calming effect on me. "We are not meant to be perfect beings; that is humanness. We are meant to be pure spiritual beings who have found one-ness with the Holiest of Holy. Essentially, we are meant to understand each day that something has happened; and it is up to us to create the next something."

"So how do I know if I am doing the right thing?" This sure seemed like the right question to be asking over and over again.

"It is what we each instill in our heart, mind, and soul that determines whether we create good or evil. In essence, we are both good and bad karmic energy as perceived by those around us." What Yeshua said made sense. My first teacher was always the best!

"It seems to me that Karma is individual to each person's vision of what karma is." I had believed this for quite some time.

"Karma is the whole of our existence. It is the mindset adopted from the beginning of our lives. If we neglect our spiritual base, we tend to become negative and as such bring about negative events. We can claim purity and piousness, but our actions must reflect that as well. We bring to our selves our pleasure or our punishment. That is the human mind speaking. Our spiritual heart can only bring joy and enlightenment. Karma is the fulfillment of all we have done... our judgment." Yeshua spoke softly and simply. "If we hurt someone, is it good or evil? If we perceive the necessity of doing something that we know might hurt someone physically, is it evil? If we lie to someone to save that person's feelings, is it good?"

"I guess it's perception." I spoke up.

"Ultimately, we must be prepared to seek balance in our deeds not based on what others think but on what we feel is spiritually correct. In the end, we must answer only for ourselves, not to men but to God. If a man chooses to walk away from war, he may very well pay in a human court but be blessed in Heaven... but what if he refuses not because of a greater truth, but because he loves no one enough to do what is asked of him? "Yeshua was in preacher mode so I sat back and listened. "If we wake each day and make a point of smiling at someone because it makes them feel good, and as such we feel good, is that good karma? What if your act is selfish because you simply want the acknowledgement of being someone sweet? If your true inner intent is not pure, your action brings bad karma in the long run. Give food, money, or shelter to someone in a truly spiritual intent, and you will be blessed; give only to appease what you think might be bad karma or to balance some wrong, and your actions will bring bad karma."

"So, a good deed is not always the good we thought it was?' I was beginning to catch on.

"All things we do must be with the purest intent. Lead someone on or lie because you haven't the courage to speak the truth, and your actions bring bad karma. Whether intentional or not, hurting someone because you fear confrontation brings bad karma. Likewise, staying in a situation you know isn't healthy simply because you do not want to hurt someone can actually be more hurtful and as such brings bad karma. 'Good' intentions do not matter. Pure intentions do." Yeshua spoke with the voice of wisdom gained from lifetimes of experience. "Whatever you do, do it honestly. It must not be deceptive or selfish or fear based. Be guided by Truth. Truth comes from your spiritual base. Only such truth can be pure. Ultimately, you must be willing to answer for all you do, but this happens at a much higher level than mere human existence."

"So, nothing is black and white. Each moment regardless of what it may appear to be has its own meaning. All I can do is adjust to each event and do my best?" I felt as though a great burden had been lifted from me.

"Exactly! Stop trying to compete with the world and become one with the universe. Accept what is and what will be. Life is simpler that way, and decisions are easier to make when you see the reality of each situation." Having said all he intended to share, he left my side.

I returned the books to the library's bin and left to take a walk. It was time to think about all I had learned and to create my future.

CHAPTER THIRTY:

Taking Charge

Adrienne and Yeshua were right about everything. It was time for me to take charge of my life. It was time for me to move forward and start creating the life I wanted. I had to stop being afraid and start being in control.

I made the decision to seek out a psychic. I figured I needed someone who at least had some idea of what I was going through. I needed a teacher. My guides were in place on the other side of the veil, but I needed someone earthbound to guide me through this part of my path.

Back in the early eighties psychics, mediums, and card readers were still considered somewhat taboo. There were not as many to be found as there are today. I couldn't even find one listed in the paper or the phone book. I decided to just drive around a few towns and see where I ended up.

It took about two weeks before I found a reader named Lillai. She had come to America after marrying an American soldier in Romania. She claimed to be a Romani gypsy and worked out of a trailer just a few miles away from Leesville, Louisiana.

I invited a friend, Maria, to come along because I honesty wasn't sure what to expect. We arrived a little after six in the evening; Lillai was ready for us. She invited us into the parlor of her centennial home and read Maria first.

I had seen Tarot readings before and knew that each reader tended to have their own style. Lillai used what is known as a Celtic cross pattern to read the cards. Her manner was kind and loving, and she was careful not to alarm my friend if anything negative came up. She was actually pretty good with the reading. Maria was amazed at many of the things Lillai had connected with.

As the reading proceeded, I noticed spirits beginning to gather around Maria. They introduced themselves to me as though I was the host of some major event. As Lillai would reveal some information, they would leave. It was as if they had come to deliver to Lillai messages for the session.

"If you are going to do that, then you need to wait outside. You are interfering with her reading!" Lillai spoke to me firmly but politely.

"Oh. Sorry. I didn't mean to." I stood to go out to the porch.

"We will talk when I am done." She smiled and motioned for me to leave.

I sat out on the porch wondering what had just happened. How did she know? I had purposely not told her anything about myself. What had I done to give myself away? I couldn't wait to talk with her!

CHAPTER THIRTY-ONE:

Lillai

After a while, it was my turn to talk with Lillai. I went back into the room and got comfortable in my chair. She poured us each a cup of tea and offered finger sandwiches. Afterwards, we both settled into our chairs. Lillai began to read me in a much different way than she had read my friend. First, she reached out and held my hands.

"For you, I am going to read your energy, your aura. The aura tells many things." She sat there for a moment to get a sense of my energy.

"What is an aura?" I had heard this term before but wasn't quite sure about it.

"The aura is the essence of your heart and soul that emanates from your body. By studying your aura, I can see into your life at this moment." Lillai acted as though I already knew this. "Now, be quiet so I can read you."

"I knew it. You are a Shadow talker. You see and hear the people in the shadows beyond this life." Lillai let go of my hands. "Why are you here? You don't need a reading?"

"I need a teacher. I don't understand all of this. Everything I do just happens." I didn't hesitate to say what I was there for.

"You cannot teach what is instinct or a natural gift... a birthright. This thing you do is a great power. It's both a gift and a curse. My people praise your gift." She acted as though I did not appreciate the gift. "You have to trust your intuition and never doubt your gift comes from a high place. Your beliefs and your attitude shape what you become."

"But, how do I focus it? How can I learn to use it the right way?" I felt like she wasn't listening to me.

"You are not listening to me. You control this. You focus it the same way you focus anything you do. Ultimately, it's up to you to decide the right way to use this. You know the difference between right and wrong." She appeared to be upset.

"I'm sorry. I'm not trying to be rude. I just don't understand how I go about doing this as a living. I mean, you have a business doing this, and I guess I want to know how to do this." I was not being clear, I suppose.

"I understand that. You have to learn two things first. Learn to trust your instincts and learn some patience. No one can teach you how to be psychic or a medium. It's a natural gift and you simply have to trust in it and use it.

It's like any ability…use it or lose it." Lillai reminded me of many school teachers I had known.

"So, basically, I just have to start doing what? Tarot readings? Ghost busting? Start holding people's hands and just babbling about whatever comes into my head?" Obviously, she was correct about my needing to learn patience.

"Your stubbornness will do more harm than good. I tell you what…I will teach you about the cards, auras, and even about the angels you bring to you. I will take you with me to gatherings and introduce you to others. In the end, it is up to you to make sense of your life and your path." She smiled and walked me to the door. "Call on me Wednesday."

Maria and I drove back to the post. Maria spent the entire trip talking about her reading and how accurate the gypsy was. I was lost in thought by the time we arrived on post. I said good night to Maria and went to my room.

CHAPTER THIRTY-TWO:

Margaret and Frank

I arrived at Lillai's house around 5 p.m. on Wednesday. She met me at the door and ushered me into her parlor. I was surprised to see that there were several women in the room. My training as a reader was about to begin.

"Ladies, this is Rod. He is a shadow talker. He is a medium." She took me into a side room where she had set up a table. On the table was a deck of Tarot cards. "I am giving these to you as a gift. After today, I want you to memorize each card and its meaning. Once you know all the cards by heart... I want you to forget about what the book says and just go with what you feel the card says."

"Um... So why am I using the cards at all?" I was a little taken back.

"The cards have greater power when they are given as a gift and you use your intuition over the general meaning of the cards. The cards offer a focus to the people you read and make it easier for them to relax. Most people associate readers with the idea they can read minds or tell the future. That is not so." For once I knew what she was talking about. "We simply have the ability to take many things into consideration to see the path a person has taken through the choices they have made."

"Ok. I get that. But, what about the visions I am having? What about the spirits that I see? What about the messages? How do I know I understand them?" My fear of failing clearly came through in these questions.

"Trust! First and foremost, never doubt what you get. Ultimately, the people you read will connect to what you give them by spirit. It doesn't have to make sense to you. As long as you keep a good heart and pure intentions, you will be guided by the spirits to deliver the right messages." Her assurance was so strong and confident; I was convinced I would do ok.

Lillai left me alone for a bit to get used to the room and such. I sat there somewhat nervously and was anxious to begin. I looked at the cards; even though I had never studied them, I felt like I would know what they said. Lillai was right... I just had to believe in myself.

The room was a smallish room lit mostly by a tiny light and several candles. The table was an old round one covered by a burgundy silk cloth and topped with two candles on opposite sides of each other. The chairs were overstuffed arm chairs upholstered with the same burgundy material as the table cloth. There was an overhead fan running quietly to cool the room. Against the wall was a smaller table with a pitcher of lemonade and cookies on it. It wasn't long before Lillai entered the room accompanied by an elderly lady named Margaret. Margaret was 82 years old but seemed younger in spirit.

"Margaret is going to be your first session. She is an old and dear friend, so treat her right." With that Lillai turned and left us alone in the room.

"Hello." I stood and held out the chair for Margaret." I will do my best."

Margaret got comfortable and accepted the glass of lemonade I offered to her. I sat for a moment and caught my breath. She smiled at me as though to say *relax*.

"Your husband passed away?" I asked, allowing myself to just say whatever came to me.

"Yes."

"His name was Frank. He called you Peggy?" It was weird. For the first time I felt as though I had some level of control over the constant flow of energy that I had always felt in the universe.

Margaret gasped, "How did you know that? Not even Lillai knows that!"

"He says you wear his hat when you sit on the porch." I was in awe of what was happening even though I realized I had been doing it all along. "Trudy is with him, and they go fishing a lot."

Margaret sat there unable to speak.

"Um…is Trudy an animal? I feel like I am seeing a dog."

"Yes. We had Trudy for almost 15 years. Frank always took her fishing with him." I noticed a tear in Margaret's eye.

"He says that he wishes he had stayed home. He didn't think it would storm." Suddenly, I realized what had happened. "Frank and Trudy drowned?"

"Yes, they got caught in a squall on the reservoir." She just stared at me with an expression that conveyed I was giving her something of the greatest value.

"He was in the military… World War One. He had a limp, and there was a burn mark on his right arm. He had trouble breathing because of the wounds he received in the war?" I was amazed at what was happening. I had suddenly become a telephone for him to send her messages.

"He had been in a major battle and was attacked by mustard gas bombs which burned him and weakened his lungs." She looked odd for a moment. "How are you doing this?"

"I'm not. He is. I'm just letting him speak." It was the only way I could think to explain it.

"Ask him what he called me; my pet name."

"Dandelion." I blushed when I realized what it meant.

"He always said I looked dandy lying in his arms." She had a mischievous grin that made me blush all the more.

"He was quite the ladies' man before we met, but he always said that I was his one and only." She smiled softly and glanced away for a moment.

"He says that he said you were his one and only sweetheart. I think he was a bit of a stickler for accuracy." We both chuckled a bit.

"He was stubborn!" She laughed.

"He is showing me a bird house?" I totally didn't have a clue what it meant.

"That was the last thing he made for me. It was for my birthday."

"He is saying Katie is with him and that she is happy and healthy." I felt both sadness and relief when I told her this.

Margaret got silent for a moment. She had a look on her face that seemed to give way to a sense of relief.

"Katie is my daughter. She developed polio and passed away when she was twelve years old. I have always wondered if she was ok." Margaret began to cry, and I must admit, so did I. "It's ok. You made me feel better. You gave me some peace."

Suddenly, I got it. I understood this gift and what it was meant for. Lillai picked Margaret for a reason. She knew I needed something this emotionally powerful for my first session. I knew my life would never be the same again.

CHAPTER THIRTY-THREE:

Outcast

"I will teach you everything I know, but in the end you are going to do this your way. I was taught by my mother in the Romani tradition. I tend to be an outcast with others who read cards. To them, I am just a crazy gypsy; but, I don't let that stop me," Lillai said. We were having breakfast at a local diner, a place I happened to love because it reminded me of a diner I used to go to in Chicago.

"I have been an outcast most of my life," I replied, "so I don't see that as being a problem. I think that no matter what I do, my destiny has always been to be different."

"True. There will always be people who laugh at what they don't understand or go on the attack because they can't do it." I could tell she had been through some tough moments as a result of choosing to be a reader.

Then I asked, "Have you ever had to deal with a spirit that seems both good and evil?" I proceeded to tell her about Pariah.

"Good and evil are perspectives to what is going on in your life. We all have to deal with our own demons sooner or later. The trick is to know the difference between a demon and our own fears. You have to figure out your own truth and be willing to accept it." Lillai spoke almost indifferently about the matter.

"That seems to be what everyone tells me in one way or another. I guess I haven't quite gotten it in my head." I was frustrated that something so apparently simple to others still seemed to be missing some level of truth for me.

"You will get it soon enough," she said; then she changed the subject. "A friend of mine hosts parties during the Mardi gras and invites various readers, psychics, and mediums to attend. We all sit in a large auditorium, and people pay 10 dollars to talk with us for 15 minutes. It's a good way to get comfortable with people and learn different ways to read people. I have permission for you to come along if you would like."

I have to admit, all I really heard was "Mardi Gras" and "parties" so I was happy to accept her invitation. I thought it would be nice to visit Adrienne's grave and maybe say hello to her grandma. It had been a while since I had been to New Orleans and felt it was time to return.

CHAPTER THIRTY-FOUR:

Constantine and Euchre

The town of Metairie, Louisiana is just outside of New Orleans. We stayed at what had to be the oldest Howard Johnson Hotel in America. From the plastered walls to the 1940's tile in the bathroom, it wore its age as one might expect from the surrounding area. I noticed the smell of moss and age which seemed to breeze in all the way from Lake Ponchartrain.

We decided to stay at the hotel that day and avoid the madness of trying to move around the French Quarter; especially Bourbon Street. Lillai and I joined three other ladies for dinner. I was actually being given a distinct honor by being allowed to join a small gathering of Romani gypsies. That evening I learned a lot about the Romani, but only what I was permitted to know; I am sure!

Two of the ladies at our table, Mala and Tarana, had similar backgrounds because they were both married to veterans, but the husbands were veterans of different wars.

The ladies' ages ranged from Lillai who was nearly 60 to Tarana who was around 30. Mala was 47 and seemed to be a bit of a historian. She would only share with me what she was allowed to, but she did tell me an interesting story about the history of Tarot Cards.

"The Tarot cards; everyone claims they are something else than what they are. Did you know that we got Tarot cards because of Constantine? The emperor that "created" a unified Christian religion; or so he thought." Mala was skilled in the art of storytelling. "Constantine ruled that there would be only one religion celebrated under his rule, and that religion was what we know as Christianity. He ordered the destruction of anything connected to other beliefs and began to persecute those who continued to follow their own beliefs above his."

"I was taught something similar at college but a little less harsh," I commented, feeling the need to have answers above the conventional ones I had been given in school.

"Of course! History is taught by those who choose to use it to make their wrongs seem right." Mala was a little annoyed with me; I think. "The other religions began to worship in secret and do their best to continue their beliefs. The Emperor sent his soldiers out to eliminate these groups and anything they possessed of their beliefs. For years the other religions were being attacked, murdered and wiped out."

"Constantine was, basically, doing a religious purification? His idea was to simplify religion by creating one canonized faith and outlawing the rest?" I didn't sound sure of myself, but I believe I was offering my interpretation of what she was saying.

"Yes. It went on for several years until a priest came up with a unique idea. During this time there was a game created called euchre. It consisted of a series of cards that players used to gamble in a somewhat acceptable way. The priest realized that these cards could be used to pass on his beliefs." Mala stopped a moment to sip her chicory coffee and eat a beignet. "The priest hired an artist to illustrate the more important doctrine of his religion on the actual cards used for euchre. In this way, he could hold a religious service using the cards, and if the soldiers were to interrupt, the people could pretend they were playing euchre."

"I've never heard this before. How do you know this information? I've never seen anything about the history of Tarot cards in books." I was genuinely curious as to the validity of this story.

"In the years ahead you will find that true history will be written and that what we have been taught is not accurate, at all," Mala smiled. "I would rather value traditional folklore over "modern doctrine" any day. Men lie. History is written by the conquerors."

"So modern day Tarot Cards descended from various religions that used euchre decks to give secret sermons to avoid prosecution from Constantine's soldiers?" This certainly was food for thought! I didn't know then that I would hear this theory several more times throughout my life.

CHAPTER THIRTY-FIVE:

Laissez le Bon Temps Rouler

Laissez le bon temps rouler... "Let the good times roll." I heard this phrase continuously during the Mardi Gras festival. I had been to two previous celebrations and loved them both! The people, costumes, parades, and energy of this particular festival was unique to anything I had ever experienced.

We arrived by bus at what seemed to be a major event hall on Canal Street just at the entrance to Bourbon Street. The room had been set up by one of the many "krewes" or groups connected to the celebration. Each krewe symbolized one thing or another. We were part of what is now referred to as a "psychic fair."

I found my table located in the back of what was a crescent moon pattern of equally spaced tables. Lillai was to my left and Mala to my right. Towards the other side of the room, I saw venders selling stones, lotions, tinctures and such. A buffet and an open bar were set up in a room off the event room. Another room contained a dance floor and a jazz band. Once we had all found our assigned places, we grabbed a bite to eat and waited for the revelers with the parade to find their way in.

People began to slowly flow into our room dressed in costumes and bringing with them high energy. The hostess sat at a table in front, and as each person walked up to her, she would assign them a reader. Slowly the tables began to fill in a way that seemed designed to give the first people to the readers who had participated before. I watched as individual readers greeted people interested in what was to be offered. I noticed how each reader seemed to do things differently. I listened in when I could just to learn how each reader communicated their gift. Finally, it was my turn.

"Hello," I stood, smiled, and greeted a middle aged woman dressed as Marie Antoinette. "Please have a seat."

We had been instructed to do fifteen minute simple card reading, so I decided to do a ten card spread. It was a rather simple reading for the woman, and she walked away happy. I looked around a bit more and waited for another person to be sent my way. I was pleasantly surprised when I saw a familiar face being sent over.

"Gary? Oh my goodness! It's good to see you!" I had met Gary and his partner John a few years earlier. They had been living in an old apartment that was "haunted" by the author Tennessee Williams.

"I saw you over here and asked if they would let me see you." Gary seemed tired but managed a smile. It was then that I went into a semi trance. I had not focused to do so; it just automatically happened.

"Gary, I am so sorry for your loss. John seemed like a really good person." Suddenly, I found myself just watching my interaction with Gary, like a part of my brain took over and pushed me to the side. "I get a sense that he drowned? I mean, I feel like his lungs are full of water."

"He got pneumonia. He'd been sick for a bit, and then he just kept getting worse," Gary informed me.

"He isn't the only one you lost. I feel like there were two others... they had almost the same thing." I didn't know exactly what I was sensing. It seemed as though some ailment had attacked Gary's friends.

"The doctors said it was something to do with their immune systems. John was fine until a year ago. Then he kept losing weight and couldn't sleep." I could tell that Gary's heart was so heavy. It was then that I noticed something in his aura.

I saw black splotches all around him. The colors I had usually associated with the aura were darker and duller than normal. His eyes seemed to be slowly emptying even as we sat there.

"John is on the other side. He is with you. I'm supposed to tell you to keep your appointment." I just accepted and conveyed the messages as they came. "He says you need to stop being so stubborn."

"Ha! Leave it to the pot to call the kettle black." Gary seemed to get a kick out of John's message.

"He says that he likes what you did with his typewriter, but the flowers are a little too much." In my head I saw what appeared to be a little shrine on a writing desk made up of an old typewriter and a wreath of flowers.

"Tell him, too bad. That's for me not him!" Gary had a warm grin on his face but a touch of sadness in his eyes.

"He says he woke you up this morning at 2:25 just to say hello." I had heard of this phenomenon happening to others as well.

"Oh my Lord! He DID! I woke up and looked at the clock. It was 2:25 a.m.!" Gary flashed a big smile.

"Thank you! You have no idea how much this means to me!" Gary stood and gave me a hug. As he walked away, I saw Death waiting for him by the door. I was going to call to him and tell him to live each day…

"He already knows." I turned around and saw that Pariah was sitting in my chair.

"You always show up when someone is dying!" I hated him but had come to realize he was not going away.

"Hell, I'm always around. You just never notice unless I talk." I hated his sarcastic tone.

"Then just shut up, and we never have to see each other!" I did not hide my disdain for him.

"Whether you acknowledge me or not... I am always near. The worse the event the stronger I am. You will never be rid of me. You just don't get it." With that he gave a sardonic laugh and vanished.

The rest of the event was fairly typical. I had been told that once everyone began to drink we would simply do standard readings, and then at 9 p.m. we would leave. I was more than ready to go. Mala, Lillai and I decided to walk down to the river and replenish our energy. This had been my first experience under such conditions. I had found it somewhat claustrophobic.

CHAPTER THIRTY-SIX:

Voodoo Wedding

After we sat along the river we decided to visit some of the shops in Jackson Square. I couldn't wait to visit Marie LaVeau's Shop and hopefully talk to her great granddaughter.

We got to the shop as it was closing. They normally stayed open later, but on this particular evening they were celebrating a wedding. We managed to catch a woman named Julianna as she was closing the door. She had met Lillai years earlier and seemed happy to see her again. After a cordial hug, Julianna asked if we would like to attend the wedding. Lillai accepted for us, and we were on our way.

We walked to Louis Armstrong Park which was some distance from the Bourbon Street district. As we arrived, we were told that "the ghetto" sprawled across the street from us occupying two sides of that area. "Drugs, crime and lost souls live there;" according to Julianna.

The ceremony was already set up and about forty people were in attendance. I could tell from the beginning that it was not like anything I had ever seen.

"You must remember that you are guest. Do not speak. No pictures may be taken. I will protect you from any bad juju or Loa's. The Priestess is stern but good. I will explain anything you want afterwards. Nothing can hurt you here, so let go of whatever you think can happen." Julianna spoke firmly but softly. "Remember; do not speak unless told to."

We found our places amongst the others. Chairs had been set up for guests, and three fires were burning near the wedding altar. There were three people standing there, two ladies and a gentleman. A young woman was playing the violin while an older gentleman played an accordion. Several women were dancing, holding onto small tambourine-like drums as though anticipating their part in the ceremony. A younger man wearing only a loin cloth and holding a coffin that measured about two feet by one foot stood in the shadows. I couldn't help but feel that there was something out of synch with this celebration.

We were forbidden to tell anyone the details of the ceremony, but it was what seemed to me a cross section of Haitian voodoo and Marie LaVeau's syncretized voodoo. What an odd mix of voodoo and Christian faith! The announcement of Gran Zombi and the various gris-gris bags were combined with the other aspects of the vodoun path.

As the ceremony ended, I was not surprised to see Azrael among the revelers. The ceremony involved so many aspects of spiritualism and the various Loa's that she had to be present. It did surprise me to see Pariah at such a joyous occasion. He looked right at me and smiled that crooked dark smile I had seen too often in my life.

As we went through the reception line and then walked away from the park, I suddenly realized why Pariah was there. The bride seemed tired and not at all certain that she had done the right thing. The groom came across as dominating and cruel. I sensed a lot of hate and anger in his energy. I realized why the event seemed out of synch... He was abusing her.

I was about to say something to Lillai when Azrael whispered in my ear..."You can't save everyone. She has a path to follow that will lead her to a happier life. First, she has to learn her way to get there. Life is filled with lessons. Sometimes we teach, sometimes we learn, and sometimes all we can do is watch."

"So we just walk away? We don't say anything?" I was angry.

"For now, it's all you can do. Someday in the future, it will change. Things must happen to create change. You can't do anything yet. I really am sorry." Azrael had never voiced any level of regret to me before about anything. "Learn from this."

Death vanished, and I found myself walking a little behind the others while I contemplated my experiences that day. My emotions seemed to be all over the place. It was somewhat defeating to know that in the same day I'd felt the pleasure of giving someone closure as well as later on the helpless anger from having to walk away from such a horrible episode. It made no sense. What kind of world exists where such things can go on?

CHAPTER THIRTY-SEVEN:

Tarana's Story

The next morning, Saturday, we had breakfast at a wonderful little café located a short walk from the hotel. I had not slept well because it had bothered me so much that I couldn't help that poor bride. It didn't seem right to just walk away. Finally, I mentioned my worry to the ladies.

"Rodney, what would you have done? Walk back and accuse the groom of abusing the bride at their wedding celebration? Do you realize what they would have done to you? He would have denied it, and she would not say a thing." Mala was trying to soothe me; I am sure. "You are young and naïve in some matters."

"If the bride was willing to go through that ceremony, then she was not ready to see his issues. She truly believes that she can change him." Lillai offered her perspective and then she looked at Tarana.

"It doesn't matter what you or anyone else would say. She will stay with him until she can see him for what he is or until he kills her." Tarana seemed to suddenly get glassy eyed. "The heart can be a cruel liar when you are in love. It can make you justify the unjustifiable."

"When I was fifteen, I dated a boy named Troy. He was my first love and my world. We met in high school and dated for years. Troy came from a family of alcoholics, but he never drank. He was so intelligent and creative. I loved him deeply." Tarana smiled at that memory, but then her smile faded. "It was in our first year of college that it began. School was overwhelming for him so he started drinking beer. He took to it like a fish in water."

"By the second half of our first year, he had joined his family in alcoholism. He even brought his flask to classes. I convinced myself that it was just a temporary way for him to relax and get through school." Tarana started to tear up a bit.

"You don't have to do this." I wanted her to know that she needn't go on. "It's ok."

"No. I need to say this for your sake. You have so much to learn, and I think my story is for you to learn from." As she spoke, I remembered Azrael telling me I would have many teachers.

"The first time he hit me, he cut my lip. I fell to the ground. Suddenly, he was over me apologizing. He swore he was sorry and it would never happen again." She paused a moment to catch her breath. "The next time he did it, he said it was my fault. He said I was asking for it. Troy was so convincing that I started to believe him."

"I stayed with him for two more years after that. I didn't leave him until five years ago when he nearly killed us both while driving to Dallas. He had gotten so drunk that he was ranting about everything and then told me he was done with life. He stared right at me and said it was entirely my fault. He said we both would be better off dead!" Lillai moved over to her and held her. "He missed the tree, but we went down an embankment. We survived the crash, but he turned on me and beat me. If people witnessing the accident hadn't gotten there when they did, he would have killed me."

"Never assume anything. Even when we know things, we do not always acknowledge it because of other reasons. We stay in bad situations even when we know better; it could be out of love, fear, or such. I do know that so many people tried to help me, but I didn't listen. I wouldn't even listen to myself." Tarana was so honest and sincere about it.

"I'm sorry that you had to go through that." I just didn't know what to say.

Tarana spoke gently to me. "Just don't punish yourself when you can't help someone. It simply means you are not the one for the job. Sometimes it takes the universe to save a soul."

CHAPTER THIRTY-EIGHT:

Changes

Over the next year or so I joined Lillai and the others for more gatherings and learned as much as I could. I sought out different people and perspectives to help me better understand my gift. The events during that time seemed almost tailor made to allow me to catch my breath and learn gentle lessons. During this time, I also had my military obligation to work as well. As I grew into my path, I found my path filled with changes.

I met a nice girl named Eleanor, and a short while later we married. Soon we added to the family. By the end of our term in service, we had two children and had decided to move to Michigan.

I said goodbye to dear friends with promises to meet again and visit here and there. Eleanor and I packed our car and with the kids in hand headed to a town called Rochester, Michigan. We had been promised jobs in the auto industry, and I also planned on working psychic fairs so I could continue to use and develop my gifts.

Upon arriving in Rochester, we were met with a phone call that informed us the jobs we had been offered were no longer available. I found myself scrambling to get a job to support us. Everything we had planned fell through and the stress was unbearable. I couldn't figure out what I had done wrong.

"What makes you think you did anything wrong?" Yeshua said to me in a dream. "Life happens. Never assume you can predict the future."

"Why is it I can read other people's futures but not my own?" I asked, finally getting to that all important question he was waiting for me to ask.

"You can't read the future; nobody can. You simply read people by the energy they put out and the decisions they make." Yeshua had never explained this to me before. "The future changes with every decision a person makes. Your gift allows you to communicate with the spiritual energy around people. When you do this and then add to it your ability to anticipate the possible outcome of a person's decision, it probably does seem a bit like seeing the future."

"So basically, I am using the ability to tap into the law of averages based on the information the spirits provide me? The cards are just a way to get people to focus on why they need to see me?" I seemed to be questioning Yeshua but had actually been constructing this explanation for some

214

time. "This also allows them to pass on messages for me to give to their loved ones?"

"Well, that's kind of a simplistic explanation, but I guess that's close enough for now." Yeshua seemed a little put off by me.

"Is something wrong?" I asked, wanting him to know I was actually attempting to read him.

"Are you really trying to read me? Ha ha! You know just when you think you understand it all, it will change." He was being a bit smug. "Seriously though... You need to lighten up. Your energy has been a little dark lately. Your life hasn't been easy. You are very different from others and have never quite fit in. That can make a person a little skeptical, maybe even a little angry."

"I am ok; just a bit frustrated by things, but I will survive it." I spoke confidently, but I wasn't sure if I was trying to convince him or myself. It just felt like every time I began feeling good about things, I had another battle to fight.

"Maybe your shift in energy is because you're being too nice about things." I knew immediately that Pariah was there but was surprised that Yeshua had gone away. "Everyone says catch your breath and be patient...Well, how is that working for you? Are you *really* any better off?"

"My life is good. I am married and have two incredible kids." I was determined to show him how wrong he was.

"There is no wrong or right in this. Do you want to take care of your children? You have a power that people need, and you deserve to be paid for it!" He struck a nerve because I had to admit that I was tired of working for minimum wage and watching my family barely get by. "Look at what some of the people at the fairs are charging, and they do not even have any real ability."

He was right about that, but I hated him for saying it! I had always promised myself I would try to charge a reasonable rate so that everyone could come see me. It just didn't seem fair that things were going the way they were. I could feel the anger inside me and didn't like it all. I knew I would have to confront it soon. I also knew I had to come to terms with Pariah and find a way to get him out of my life.

CHAPTER THIRTY-NINE:

Missing

In the spring of 1986, I was called by an old friend living in the Chicago area. Danny and Debbie had moved out to the suburbs and raised a small family. Their lives had been perfect until a few weeks ago when they got a phone call that their daughter, Lisa, had disappeared. After an exhaustive search, Danny decided to contact me and see if I might be able to locate her.

"Rod, one night she just never showed up at work, and no one has seen her since." Dan sounded exhausted.

"Dan, I've never actually used my skills to locate missing people. I usually can only connect with people who have passed away." I didn't know what else to tell him.

"Well, could you at least try? Please?" He was desperate and needed answers.

"Okay. Give me a minute to see what I can feel." I had no idea if this would work but knew I had to try.

I sat down next to the phone and just let myself go into the zone. I had no hope that this would work. I thought about when Dan and I were kids, and we all went to the old cemetery on Ela Road. Then out of the blue I saw an old Chevy pick-up truck and a drum filled with oil.

"Dan, do you know anyone who drives an old Chevy or has a garage?"

"Well, Lisa's ex-boyfriend works at a garage in a junk yard."

"Dan, is there a beat up old Chevy near the back of the garage?"

"I don't know. I can go check it though." I knew a part of him had realized what I might be thinking when he asked, "Do you think he may have hurt her?"

"I don't really know what to think. I just get this sense that the truck is important to finding her. I saw both a truck and a large drum like they use in garages to dump oil in." I probably sounded more confident than I actually was for Dan's sake. I really wasn't sure at all. I think I was hoping I was wrong more than I was right.

Dan hung up and said he would call me back as soon as possible. I lay down on the couch and tried to concentrate on finding Lisa. Suddenly, I realized that Dan's daughter was dead. Her things were dissolving in the oil drum, or so the ex was hoping...

Dan called about two hours later. "Rod, I'm at the garage. The Chevy is here, but the police say it hasn't been moved. The weeds are growing all around it."

"Dan, in my vision he lifted the car with the large crane. Is there something like that there?"

"Just a minute..." I could hear him talking to someone in the background. "Rod, there is one! An officer just noticed fresh marks and new rust on the truck suggesting it was lifted."

"Oh, my God. Seriously?" I was astounded. "Dan, can I talk to one of the officers. Please?"

I could hear the phone being passed to someone.

"Officer Logan, here."

"Hello. Officer Logan, I am not sure if Dan realizes his daughter might be dead and buried under the truck. Can you guys call someone for him to be there just in case?" I could only imagine how it was going to feel for this to fully sink in. I know I would be devastated.

"We have to get the proper paperwork to search here, so I'll make sure things are in motion for that as well." Officer Logan had obviously already realized what was going on. "You know, I don't necessarily believe in this stuff, but if you are right, then you have done a good thing for your friend. A lot of folks never get to know what happened to their kids."

"Thanks. I kind of hope I am wrong though." I hung up after I was promised I'd get an update as soon as possible.

A few hours later I received the call that they had found Lisa and that her belongings were, indeed, in the barrel of oil. I asked that my name not be mentioned. Even though I knew I might help someone find closure, I truly did not want to do that type of work again. I guess I figured the universe would send those events to me when it was my job. After all, I can't help everyone, can I?

CHAPTER FORTY:

Challenges

I decided to work full time and do readings on the weekends and at Psych Fairs even though I was not a fan of them any longer. Through the years I had found them to become overcrowded and, in a sense, nothing but tarot mills. The idea of herding people through fifteen minute card readings just didn't work for me, and I found myself unable to meet the fifteen minute deadlines. This is not to say the fairs are not good, just that I wasn't comfortable with rushing people through in hopes of having them make an appointment for a longer session at some other date.

I had come to feel that people would be guided to who they needed at a time they needed them. I knew then as I know now that we all need different teachers and guides all through our lives. This attitude did cause some animosity between some of the other readers and me. It wasn't long before I was made to feel like an outcast at these gatherings.

To make matters worse, I was asked by a local police department to help bust a group of so-called phone psychics that were essentially ripping people off with a fraudulent scheme. Apparently they had developed a "yes or no" type call sheet designed to keep people on the phone as long as possible. These phone psychics would take their time getting your credit card number and initial information; then they would begin to ask basic questions. If you said "yes" they would go to one string of questions and if you said "no," they would go to another. They were not psychic on any level, and yet their system made them seem incredible.

I applied to work for this group by way of a newspaper advertisement appearing in several papers. They hired me immediately based upon my voice and ability to talk a certain way on the phone. Those of us hired were trained on how to pick up on what people would say and then steer them in a direction that would keep them on the phone the longest. My job for the police was to go through the training and get a copy of the question chart. Getting this chart proved to be the hard part for me because at the end of each shift all charts were locked up.

I worked with the phone psychics for two weeks and did my best to keep track of the calls I handled and any personal information shared in hopes of gaining witnesses for prosecution later. The phones had been tapped. The officers even had people who would call in as clients. The police operation was amazingly well thought out, and I could see how people could be fooled. It also made me even more skeptical about the psychic industry.

The group of fake psychics was closed down on the second day of the third week I worked there, and I felt as though I had done a great thing in helping people. The police had agreed to keep my name out of this operation because I didn't want to take a chance on my family being hurt.

A few weeks later, I participated in a Psychic Fair with a friend from Detroit. She had reserved two spots, but her partner couldn't make it so she invited me. Psychic fairs had been changing more to appeal to the public and were now known as Mind, Body, and Spirit Festivals. They were becoming more commercial but still included a lot of both paranormal things and metaphysical businesses as well.

I took my reserved space and waited for the coming crowd of people seeking readings. As I sat watching the other readers approach their tables, I was shocked to see that three of the arriving readers were people who had been employed by the illegal phone operation! My thoughts went into overdrive. Would any of them recognize me? If they did, would they know I was the person who helped put them out of business?

It wasn't too long until one of them walked up to the woman who organized the event and spoke to her. They looked my way. A moment later, the event coordinator walked over to my friend and told her that I was not properly registered and could not work the event. My friend argued that she had paid for two spots and as such had a right to use her space as she felt necessary. The organizer simply returned her money and said I had to leave. Later, we learned that the gentleman who had approached her was a relative. This so-called spiritual woman did not even give me a chance. Lesson learned.

Challenges like the Detroit psychic fair situation seem to have followed me all through my life. They began shaping me early and continued to do so as I attempted once again to create my path. The world was changing; it was become somewhat darker.

CHAPTER FORTY-ONE:

Dark Times

After the Psychic Fair incident, I began to feel uneasy. At first I thought it was just anxiety from the experience, and I tried to ignore it. I worked, played games with my kids, and went about daily life as best I could. Unfortunately, my sleep patterns were broken, and insomnia ruled my dreams. The dreams began to contain Azrael, the angel of death, constantly standing in the background.

"Why are you here?" I was finally frustrated with these dreams. "Are you going to talk to me or not?"

Death stood silent.

"Why won't you tell me what's going on; who is going to die? I feel it." My heart felt like it was bursting with anxiety.

"You already know who is going to die. Why should she tell you what you already know?" Pariah's voice sounded like he had gargled glass. He stood beside me staring with his glowing black eyes. "You have always been a

Pollyanna. Thinking everything will work out in the end. Well, it's not going to."

"Shut up! Don't push me." I was tired of him and his negativity. I wanted him to leave my life!

"You have become an outcast even with people of your own ilk. You don't fit in anywhere, and it's going to get worse!" Pariah smiled as though he had just told some joke that I should understand. "Where is Yeshua? Where is your angel when you need him? When has he ever been there?" I felt badgered.

I was getting angrier and angrier at this rabid dog of a creature. I kept calling out to Yeshua for guidance, but I heard nothing. My emotions were raw, and my heart filled with darkness. I knew I had reached a low point when I actually started believing that Pariah was right about Yeshua.

"Of course, I'm right!" Pariah stood almost in triumph.

"No. You are not right. All you ever do is let me know when something bad is going to happen. You are a harbinger of bad things." I hated him, and yet... I didn't send him away; I'd never sent him away, even after I'd learned how.

"Whatever, you know who is dying, and you can't do anything about it. You just have to watch, hope and pray that you are wrong." His smugness was unbearable. "All you can do is wait patiently and watch as it happens. That's some gift you have…"

Suddenly, I woke up in a sweat and knew that Pariah was right and all I could do is wait. All I would be able to do is stand by and hope that I was wrong.

CHAPTER FORTY-TWO:

Losing My Religion

The next evening, my father called to tell me that my mom had been diagnosed with Leukemia. They had been preparing to retire to Arkansas when she started feeling off. I was crushed. I had sensed it, but hoped I was wrong. I was not.

My thoughts went back to when I was nine years old, when the doctor stood over me and told Mom that I was going to die, and she told him she wouldn't let me die. All I knew was that I couldn't do the same for her. She was going to die, and nothing I could do would change that.

"I am sorry." Azrael finally decided to speak to me. "The universe has a synchronous pattern that cannot be broken...for anyone."

"Sorry? You're sorry?" My anger burst forward. "You knew, and you didn't say anything. Would a few hours have made a difference?"

"Everyone dies. You lived because you have things to do and people to help. Your mother has almost finished her purpose here.' Azrael offered some odd logic, but I didn't want to hear it. "You should know that when she leaves she will have…"

"Shut up! Shut the fuck up!!!" All I felt was hate and anger. "I trusted you. You let me live so let her live. Take me. I don't want to lose my mom!"

"I can't. This is how it has to be." Death sought to embrace me, but I backed away.

"Leave! I don't ever want to see you again until my final moment. I don't need your sympathy or your guidance!" With that I put up a strong wall to prevent her from being around me, and she was gone. If I could have made her hurt like I did, I would have done it!

"Was that necessary?" Yeshua asked, appearing with Pariah at his side. "We have talked about this. Ultimately, Death is a part of the universe that brings everyone to final judgment. She rarely shows herself to anyone until that last moment. She connected to you. You gave her some level of humanity."

"I don't care. If she truly "connected" to me, she would not take my mom!" I raged. "And, how about you? You saved *me* so why not *her*? Trade me for her."

"You know it doesn't work that way. People have a certain lifespan. Some live longer than others because they have different lessons. No one is allowed to go past their time...their fate." Yeshua talked *so* calmly that it simply angered me more.

"So, you didn't save *me*? You let *me* get hurt and nearly die! Is this some sick game?" I had reached my breaking point. "I am done with you, too. I never asked for any of you to be in my life. Just leave me alone!"

Yeshua looked at me for a moment, then left. I stood there huffing and wanting to scream as loud as I could. This was my reward for *accepting* my gift? I felt betrayed.

"Of course you were betrayed. You have been lied to and manipulated all along. Now, you are an outcast. Everything you ever hoped for will always be interrupted by this gift. "Pariah slithered up to me as though he were drawn to my hate and anger. "How does it feel to realize your life is a lie? You struggled to find some spiritual place that never existed and now you are going to lose one of the most important people in your life. That's all they have done is take the people you care about. You owe them nothing!"

"I don't owe anyone anything! I am done." I finally realized it was time for me to live my life for me. "You disgust me. You need to go too!"

"You can't get rid of Yeshua or me. We are a part of you. Eventually, you will decide what you have to, but you can't rid yourself of who you are. Good and evil are not what you think. The only true balance to them is Death, and you have forbidden her from your life." Pariah began to laugh.

I just stopped feeling anything at this point. I looked at Pariah, and I used my will to push him deep within my subconscious. I caught my breath, and for a moment…everything ceased to exist. I was at the foot of a great mountain walking towards a cabin. And then everything went dark…

At this point, I had decided to work as a medium full-time and hold part-time jobs to round things out financially. Since I had buried my so-called guides, I decided to start over and do things my way. No more Psychic Fairs or allowing anyone to disrespect me. I didn't need friends. I didn't need partners. I didn't need Faith.

I had a hell of a gift, and it was time to use it my way. No more rules just do and say what I felt appropriate, regardless. I was at a point to where if people didn't like it, then to hell with them. I was more than happy to be an outcast. I was more than happy to be a pariah.

CHAPTER FORTY THREE:

The Last Saint Patrick's Day...

"You are going to visit your mom?" Adrienne asked, walking with me through the woods.

"Yes, I promised her I would year ago," I replied, thinking that I walked through the woods along the river a lot these days.

"You are meeting her in Chicago along the river?" Adrienne continued, always there when I needed her. In those days, I didn't seem to have too many people in my life.

"Yep, it's Saint Patrick's Day, and we always celebrate together," I said. Then I began to tell Adrienne about how my mom and I came to celebrate St. Paddy's each year.

"When you are raised in an Irish Catholic family, in an Irish Catholic neighborhood in Chicago, you tend to see St. Paddy's Day a little differently than most." I faded off a little into memories of my past. "First of all, as a kid you learn to breathe differently on that day because everyone's house smells of cornbeef and cabbage."

"Hahaha! Oh, my goodness!" Adrienne laughed at my scrunched up face of disdain for cornbeef and cabbage. "You are so funny!"

"Very often as a child I'd wished that a Jewish kid would move into the neighborhood so I could hide from that noxious aroma on St. Pat's Day! If you've never had the joy of cornbeef and cabbage, then be warned that it isn't as good as they want you to think. It's worth a try, but only for the reason to say you tried it. My opinion has always been something this side of *Yuck!* The word *cabbage* has always sounded too much like garbage to me, and when it's cooked enmasse, it smells too much like it as well!" Reflecting back, I suppose to the twelve year old me, it did indeed seem that way.

"In the early morning, you raced to the Chicago River to watch as the river began its emerald transition and eventual journey snaking throughout the city. It isn't St. Pat's until someone turns it liquid green. Rivers, beer, and in some cases rivers of beer flowed continuously. Around noon, my Mom and Grandmother would dress us up in our finest Sears and Roebuck suits and march us off to the eternal condemnation of St. Pat's Mass. I realize now that my memories of these masses lasting well into the next year are not quite accurate, but still they seem awfully close. The men of the house were allowed temporary redemption due to the fact that my Uncle Milton needed all hands on deck at his bar and restaurant once located off Michigan Avenue. How I loved to remember those magical days!

"Uncle Milton's mighty Irish Rednecks served as beer tenders, waiters, chefs, and bouncers. Throughout the day, the *wanna-be* Irish were served commercial grade green beer, C&C, and canned Irish music. After nine o'clock, the bar closed to become a very Irish Family gathering. If there wasn't at least one fight by 9:15, Uncle Milton would often get one started. Punching was a great part of this holiday. Milton had an unofficial ring set up in a backroom to handle such indelicacies." I struck an old style boxing pose, and Adrienne giggled at me.

"The women would stomp in with arms full of various cornbeef and cabbage recipes ranging from spicy to sweet. They would bring potato bread and salt pork and other lesser known Irish fare. Then the real music would start! Danny Gale played a fiddle like no one else could, and Donnie Odonnel would raise his squeezebox in triumph while belting out an old Irish Jig. The Robertson Clan would struggle to play everything from spoons and tables to metal drum serving trays. Not a musical bunch at all..." But these memories always made me smile.

I remember watching my sisters and cousins dance ethnic twirls and modern variations. Some people came in costumes, but most came to drink, brag and just plain have a good time.

"Through it all, my mother would sit and watch and smile and laugh. She would dance a bit, drink a wee bit, and wisp in and around the various guests making sure they had their fill of food and drink. Mom loved St. Pat's as much as some people like Halloween or Christmas! She loved family and the great gatherings that come with it." I paused, wiping away the slight tear in my eye.

"As time wore on, the gatherings grew smaller and the glad tidings came further apart. I remember once taking my mom to coffee in the morning on St. Pat's. She began to talk about those happy days, and I noticed a warm smile on her face and a soft tear in her eye. She told me that no matter what, she would always celebrate St. Pat's... even if she had to do it alone. I tried very hard to make sure she never celebrated alone. Some years we would sneak off for pie at a local diner, but oddly enough end up at a place called Sweet Nellie's for a "wee" bit of joy!" I felt happy telling Adrienne about this wonderful time I got to share with my mother.

In 1986, Mom was diagnosed with Luekemia. They gave her 30 days. Her reaction... she smiled and said *I will go when I'm ready.* However, I saw that soft tear again that told me her days were dwindling down.

I was determined to spend St. Pat's with Mom in 1987. We followed tradition; driving to Chicago and watching the river run green. By this time, Uncle Milton's bar was long gone and the building itself replaced, so we found a nice little place that did its best to serve up C&C, but Mom could always tell store bought.

My thoughts were briefly interrupted! "You need to spend time with her for your sake. I don't like this angry person you are becoming!" Adrienne told me, never failing to be honest.

I had gone to Chicago that year to share St. Pat's Day with my mother, and I ended up dancing with her on a bridge over the Chicago River, just because... As we danced and folks looked on, the river ran emerald and the sky allowed the sun to rain down upon us. I promised Mom we would do it again next year. She smiled that beautiful smile, the smile that so often gave me the strength and courage to live my life and be proud of whom I am! And then I saw that soft tear that she so often tried to hide. I knew this was our last Saint Patrick's Day.

CHAPTER FORTY FOUR:

A Visit from Mom...

In the days leading up to her death, I had tried not to be angry, but her forthcoming death was the last straw for me. So many people I loved were leaving my life in one way or another. My heart was filling with anger and shutting down. This gift I had was a curse. I hated it and decided that I was done. It was time to call it quits and "get a real job."

Mom passed away on Saint Patrick's Day in 1988. We never again danced on the bridge nor did we share a "wee bit" of joy. We did, however, have a warm and beautiful talk.

"Wake up!" I opened my eyes and was happily startled to find Mom waking me up. "We need to talk."

"Mom?" It took me just a moment to realize that I was having a visitation. Before I knew it, I blurted out, "You died."

"I am passing. I want to talk to you before I go." She was standing at the foot of my bed, wiggling my big toe. When

I was a kid, this was always her way of telling me I was going to be ok. Then she said, "I don't like the way you are dealing with things. Choosing to be angry and negative isn't going to help or change anything."

I sat up in bed as she sat down at the foot of the bed.

"When you were about a week away from being born, you almost died, and I prayed that you would be ok. The doctors were all amazed when you suddenly gained strength and your heart beat became strong. I knew right then and there it was because you had so much love to bring to this world." Her smile at me filled the room with light. "I swear you hit the ground running from the moment you were born.

"You always seemed to know when someone needed a hug or just needed your comforting presence and a smile," Mom said with pride. Then she continued, "You are going to lose faith through the years, but you will never lose your spirituality."

"Mom, can't I give you some extra energy or something? I don't want to lose you, too!" I so wanted to find out that there was some secret thing I could do; after all, I am a healer, right?

"We all have a fate to meet. My life was so full. I raised amazing children and got to see my grandchildren. I got to travel all over and see so many things that I never thought I would." She was smiling again. "I wish I didn't have to leave, but we all have different lifetimes. I am going to be okay. I am going to see my daddy again and my sisters.

"Life is going to throw some tough times at you and the world. More and more, people are going to give up and walk away. This world needs people who will be there to offer some hope. They will need someone that really does care and is willing to be an outcast if need be." She looked deep into my soul. "You are human, and it's okay that there will be times when you really don't want to do what you do.

"Your life is never going to stop changing. There will always be someone who needs your help, but you have to also remember to live your life too." Mom knew I needed to hear this. "Oh and there will always be stupid people who think they are clever when they say... Did you say *psychic* or psycho? Just remember, they are seriously either jealous or scared of what you do. "

Mom went on to tell me many other things that I would forget when I awoke, but I would remember what she said when the time came for me to know and use the information. We talked a little longer, and then she had to leave.

"Your dad is waiting at the hospital with me, and it's time for me to leave. He is going to have a rough time of it this week, and you need to let go of your anger towards him. I love you and have always believed in you. Don't let the harshness of this world take away your light. You have a lot to do in this lifetime." She smiled, wiggled my toe, and softly faded away.

I remembered whispering, "I love you, Mom," as I gently fell into sleep.

The phone rang around 6 a.m. It was my brother Larry calling to tell me that Mom had passed away. I thanked him for letting me know and then went and hugged both of my children on and off for most of the morning.

I took a short walk down the dirt road we lived on to catch my breath. As I reached the small clearing by the river, it didn't surprise me that I was met by Adrienne and Yeshua. Mom had shown me that I could never close my heart off to them. In fact, as we walked, I looked down the way into the shade of an old barn by the road and I saw Pariah. He was doing what he does best... standing there...in the shadows darkly lit.

EPILOGUE:

...Endings

The lightening strikes and thunder awakened me from my memories. Blood Alley was filled to the brim and the Deliverers of souls were beginning to arrive. Over the years Pariah had grown weary of his task and I could see that his time was almost at an end. I wondered; who will replace him? I never really learned much about him.

Yeshua, as always, glowed with angelic power to attract the truly righteous and pure. Azrael stood near. She was watching over the crowd like some great conductor seating her passengers for their ride; being sure to seat them in order of their exit from this journey. I stood there as each soul I had attracted as a beacon released itself to join its guide.

The rain began to falter and soon became a soft mist in the slowly emerging light of the full moon rising. The alley slowly began to empty as each spirit went about its way. From the mist one more guide emerged to collect her souls waiting to move on. These were very special souls that need a very special guide.

It did not surprise me when Adrienne decided that she would be a Deliverer. I had always expected her to do exactly as she had done. Adrienne was a mothering spirit

241

and, as such, who was better suited to gather the children? She came over to me and smiled.

"Hey, gorgeous!" Adrienne was still able to make me feel better. "I spoke to your mom the other day and she said to tell you she loves you. She says for you to take it easy and slow down a bit. I agree with her!" Adrienne was never one to mince words.

"Tell her I said hello. I will slow down soon enough." I knew that she knew these were just words. This had become my life. It was the only thing I knew how to do.

"We worry about you. She is such a wonderful woman. I can see her in you. "Adrienne could not have said anyting more complimentary to me than that. "You need to go visit your dad. You should talk to him more."

"I know. I just wish that he and I could talk to each other. He doesn't like what I do." I really did wish he and I had a better relationship.

"He loves you. He just doesn't know how to talk to you because he doesn't really understand you. You are a lot like him; you know." She gave a bit of an impish grin at that little bit of revelation.

"Hell. I look just like him." I smiled at that because I had always vowed to NEVER be like him. "I love him too. I will call him."

"I have to go now. These children have a wonderful adventure ahead of them and some are going to go back in a very short time." Adrienne always seemed to glow when she knew she had spirits that would get to come back so soon. She always said that children need as many chances as they can get. " Well, It's time. I love you so very much."

"I love you too. I miss you." Before I could say another word she kissed me softly; wiped away my tear and vanished into the night with her children in tow. The soft gentle touch of her gossamer kiss lingered on my lips.

I walked away slowly heading down the alley towards the Goodman Theater marquee. As I passed the stage door to the Oriental Theater I glanced a moment at Eddie Foy who was still at his post. We looked at each other for a moment and I quietly offered him passage to the other side. He smiled, checked to be sure that all of his audience had finally found their way and slowly faded into the beyond.

The rain had finally given way to a warm moonlit evening. The full moon seemed to smile at the earth and I felt good. I was content with my place in the universe. My ability was as much a curse as it was a gift; but then, isn't that life?

Made in the USA
Middletown, DE
26 September 2015